More Ways to Handle
the Paper Load

More Ways to Handle the Paper Load

On Paper and Online

Edited by

Jeffrey N. Golub

National Council of Teachers of English
1111 W. Kenyon Road, Urbana, Illinois 61801-1096

Manuscript Editor: L. L. Erwin
Staff Editor: Bonny Graham
Interior Design: Doug Burnett
Cover Design: Pat Mayer

NCTE Stock Number: 32103

It is the policy of NCTE in its journals and other publications to provide a fo-rum for the open discussion of ideas concerning the content and the teaching of English and the language arts. Publicity accorded to any particular point of view does not imply endorsement by the Executive Committee, the Board of Directors, or the membership at large, except in announcements of policy, where such endorsement is clearly specified.

Every effort has been made to provide current URLs and e-mail addresses, but because of the rapidly changing nature of the Web, some sites and addresses may no longer be accessible.

Library of Congress Cataloging-in-Publication Data

More ways to handle the paper load : on paper and online / edited by Jeffrey N. Golub.
    p. cm.
   Includes bibliographical references.
   ISBN 0-8141-3210-3 (pbk)
  1. English language—Composition and exercises—Study and teaching (Secondary)—United States. 2. High school teachers—Workload—United States. 3. Grading and marking (Students)—United States. 4. Group work in education. I. Golub, Jeffrey N., 1944– II. National Council of Teachers of English.
   LB1631.M597 2005
   808'.042'0712—dc22

                                            2005000071

Contents

Introduction

I still remember an incident several years ago when I was teaching at Shorecrest High School in Seattle, Washington. I had just entered my classroom to begin my fifth-period class. My conference period had just ended and a colleague, who used my classroom during Period 4, was gathering up her stuff to leave: her briefcase, a plastic crate of instructional materials, and a pile of student papers—a giant, jumbled, teetering stack of papers. As she passed me at the door, she rolled her eyes and muttered, "There's got to be a better way."

It was exactly that concern that prompted the NCTE Classroom Practices Committee in 1979 to issue a call for manuscripts and subsequently publish a volume on the topic of *How to Handle the Paper Load*. Over the years, that book has continued to be in high demand for the simple reason that the problem of overload has never gone away. It was a problem then, and it's a problem now. I was a member of the original committee that solicited, reviewed, and selected the articles for the 1979 volume, so I was pleased when Zarina Hock, NCTE's Senior Editor, called and invited me to produce an updated, "new and improved" anthology of articles on the same subject.

So what has changed in the years since the first volume was published? Well, unfortunately, not much. If anything, the pressures are even greater in this era of overcrowded classrooms, federal and state mandates, teacher shortages, testing, and budget cuts. Indeed, as every contributor to this current anthology makes clear, the problem is still very much with us.

And, further, in our information age a new aspect of writing instruction has emerged, one that was not at all present when the first volume was published in 1979: the electronic paper load. In Dennis Baron's words, we have all progressed from pencils to pixels, reaping the benefits of the new technology of writing. Students are increasingly using instructional technology as an aid to writing instruction, creating digital portfolios, handing in their assignments by posting them on their course Web sites, getting electronic feedback from both teachers and classmates. So I have included a whole section of articles in this volume that details creative, efficient, and worthwhile ways to handle this new dimension: the digital paper load.

But, while the paper-load problem remains with us, so, too, do certain solutions—certain principles and practices—that can help us to conduct frequent and productive writing instruction and still handle the resultant paper load efficiently and effectively. The contributors to this volume offer exemplary classroom practices. Let me summarize some of their insights here:

- One learns to write by writing.

  The authors of these articles do not control the paper load by shying away from writing instruction. Instead, they recognize that students must engage in some kind of writing almost daily if their written performance with language is to improve.

- Students should practice writing for a wide variety of audiences and purposes.

  The writing that students do is not limited to the all-American five-paragraph expository essay. Instead, teachers engage students in "writing-to-learn" activities that encourage them to reflect deeply on their learning and on the improvements in their written language performance. Additionally, students have frequent opportunities to write in forms that span the universe of discourse. Different audiences and purposes demand differences in style, word choice, and organization, and students should experience a wide variety of these elements. The articles in this volume will expand your repertoire of appropriate and diverse writing exercises and formats that you might use with your students.

- *Audience* is everything.

  Students will write when they have an audience for their writing. Kind of makes sense, doesn't it? Think for a moment of the messages you hear on your telephone's answering machine: do you notice how stiff and stilted and monotone the voices sound? That's because the caller is talking into a dead phone—there is really no one on the other end of the line at the moment he or she is leaving the message. And when you direct your students to write without your providing them an audience for their written efforts, you are asking them, in effect, to speak into a "dead" phone.

  You, the teacher, by the way, cannot serve as an authentic audience for students' writing. You're not *real* to the students—at least, not as real as their classmates. So it is important to let the students know that their writing will be read by their classmates. And, for much of their writing, you can also put them into imaginary situations where they have a wide variety of audiences to "speak" to. Many of the articles in this volume describe classroom designs and structures that make the provision of audience an integral part of the instructional procedure.

- Collaborative writing and peer-reviewing strategies are encouraged.

  Several articles in this volume describe a variety of procedures for collaborative writing and peer-review activities, and you should find them especially valuable. Collaborative writing offers students the opportunity to try out their "rough-draft" thoughts on an attentive audience. Working in pairs or small groups to complete an assignment is not cheating; it's learning. It's using one's own talk as a vehicle for learning and understanding and reflecting. A side benefit of collaborative writing, by the way, is that it cuts the teachers' paper load in half.

  Since much of writing is *re*writing, it is important to develop students' abilities to engage in peer reviewing of papers. Students are learning what to look for, what works (and doesn't work). Teachers are getting over the idea that they are the only ones who can provide helpful, pertinent, valuable feedback. The students themselves can provide this service for their classmates; they just need to learn some basic procedures and insights. The articles in this volume will describe how to make this kind of learning happen in your classroom.

- Teachers do not need to grade (or even read) every piece of writing that their students produce.

  The idea that we must read and grade each and every written assignment is one of teachers' most stubbornly held beliefs: "If I assign it, then I've got to read it; and if I read it, I've got to mark it up and/or grade it." But students don't necessarily want or need grades on their work. What they really want instead is an audience and feedback.

The contributors here describe several ways to incorporate these most important elements into one's writing instruction. They describe a wide variety of worthwhile assignments and activities that need an audience, not a grade, to be effective. They detail procedures for collaborative writing and peer reviewing that allow students to respond to their classmates' writing efforts, offering their classmates both an appreciative audience and substantive, pertinent feedback.

The use of instructional technology, moreover, provides for a sense of audience in wonderfully immediate and vivid ways. The contributors who talk about handling the *electronic* paper load describe collaborative efforts among whole classrooms of students in different states. The senses of time and space disappear while, at the same time, the immediacy of one's audience becomes paramount through students' electronic exchanges.

These, then, are some of the insights you will gain and procedures you will learn more about to help you manage your paper load. Good teaching is knowing the options available to you, and the articles in this volume will greatly expand your repertoire of worthwhile options, which will have you engaging your students in writing daily and still handle the resultant paper load efficiently. You're about to get some real help with a real problem that should become real manageable real soon.

Jeffrey N. Golub
Seattle, Washington

Work Cited

Baron, Dennis. "From Pencils to Pixels: The Stages of Literacy Technologies." *Passions, Pedagogies, and Twenty-First Century Technologies.* Ed. Gail E. Hawisher and Cynthia L. Selfe. Logan: Utah State UP; Urbana, IL: NCTE, 1999. 15–33.

I Ideas for Classroom Practices, Procedures, and Portfolios

1 Handling the Paper Load: Three Strategies

Barbara A. Mezeske
Hope College

Exiting the school building at the end of a long Friday, a high school English teacher lugs a briefcase bulging with poetry journals from his sixty tenth graders, each of whom has written three times a week for the past four weeks. In addition, he carries a batch of familiar essays from the creative writers. These will join the half-read stack of tests sitting on his desk at home. The weekend looks bleak.

A college composition instructor gazes up from the pile of draft essays she has been reading. They were submitted yesterday afternoon, and if she wants to get them back to students by tomorrow's class, she must keep reading. However, it's already 11:00 p.m., and she has an early class. The students will just have to wait until next week.

A veteran teacher, plowing his way through a set of essays on American literature, glances at his watch. If he allows ten minutes per paper, he will be finished in five hours. This leaves room for only limited written comments— most often a summary comment at the end of the paper, plus red marks for the most egregious errors.

All of us have seen these things happen; most of us have been there.

No one in the profession disputes the value of writing assignments. Writing is, after all, how we learn to think: it forces us to articulate, organize, and clarify our thoughts. Writing requires mental engagement, and we know that learning is most effective when the learner is engaged. Logically, then, more writing is better for students.

At the same time, writing is always produced for an audience. Most of the time, students regard their teachers as their most important audience (i.e., the ones who give the grades). Even when we use a variety of peer-review strategies and ungraded in-class writing, students need to be accountable to their teachers for the quality of writing they produce in order to produce their best. Moreover, we teachers need to read what we assign in order to gauge the value of our assignments, to assess the progress students are making, and to make choices about our next activities. Yet if we read our students' work rapidly and superficially, we are less able to offer thoughtful feedback and more likely simply to *grade* rather than to *respond* to our students' work.

Is it possible to manage an ambitious paper load and retain the value of writing assignments? Yes! Here are three strategies that work whether the teacher is working online or with paper copies. Practiced in combination or singly, these strategies will reduce the amount of time teachers spend reading papers, focus their reading so that feedback is more effective, and level out the usual roller-coaster flow of papers that comes across teachers' desks.

Engage students in written dialogue about their writing. Usually when we read student work we feel compelled to consider every element: idea, organization, development, mechanics. We look at the forest, and also at each individual tree, bogging ourselves down with so much that we want to say, yet so little time (and space at the bottom of the page) in which to say it. An alternate strategy is to ask students to participate in the feedback process, giving us some guidance about where to focus our attention. I ask students to write me a note on the back of their papers responding to one of several prompts: "What is the strongest section of this paper, and why?" "What rhetorical strategies have you used to develop your argument? What makes them effective?" "What section of your paper is the weakest, and what might you do to improve it, if you had time?" "Where have you used thick description [or any other technique you wish to highlight] and how did it work?" As students become accustomed to reflecting on their written work, the questions can become more open: "What is the best element of this paper?" "What is the weakest element?" "What do you want me to notice, especially?"

Then, when I read the papers, I begin with the writers' comments, allowing their expressed concerns to guide both my attention and my written feedback. The backs of their papers thus become an exchange of personal notes: the students tell me what they are most concerned about and I respond to their concerns. My readings of the papers are focused in a meaningful way, and because the students themselves have participated in creating that focus, my comments are more likely to be taken seriously. Since I am no longer reading a paper to make a global response to all its elements, I am able to proceed faster. Additionally, because this strategy asks students to make metacognitive responses to their own writing, they become better equipped to comment on their own and peers' writing at other points in the semester.

Read selectively, based on choices you and your students make. I like to make journal assignments because journal writing is less formal than drafted writing, more spontaneous in subject, and less guarded in tone. Journal writing is like practicing a sport: even though there is only one football contest per week, the players are on the field every day, rehearsing their moves. My journal assignments span several weeks or even the entire length of a course and require students to write two or more times a week. A journal assignment can generate an enormous amount of writing. Is it important to read every word?

Maybe not. Just as coaches watch players selectively during practice, we can read selectively and still maintain our standards. Imagine that journals are due at the end of the third week of class. Thirty students, writing three times a week, have produced 270 journal entries. A teacher can decide how many journals she is prepared to read. Three per student? Four? Perhaps five? She asks students to select one or more entries; she will randomly choose the rest. This dramatically reduces the teacher's reading load, invites students to participate in the evaluation process, and makes substantive feedback possible.

Stagger due dates. Most teachers remember the week when they found they had inadvertently scheduled the submission of major papers from every class they taught. Most of us were novices when that happened. Many of us, however, still bury ourselves under paperwork whenever due dates occur. Our students' papers come to us in *batches* or *stacks*. I suggest that a *steady stream* of paperwork is easier to manage.

This is easy with journal assignments: simply assign students to groups and then give each group different due dates so that papers come in each week or even each class session. Say that I have thirty students in a twice-a-week literature class, and each student writes one page, once a week. I divide them into six groups of five students. At *each class meeting*, I collect one group's work. During the first week, groups 1 and 2 turn in one paper each. During the second week, groups 3 and 4 turn in 2 papers each. In week 3, groups 5 and 6 turn in 3 papers each. By the seventh class session, I am back to groups 1 and 2. At the end of twelve weeks, I will have read 360 papers, but never more than 15 short papers at once.

Staggered due dates can also work with more conventional paper assignments, if we are willing to introduce variability into the kind of work our students do in class. We must begin by deciding whether it is important for students to be learning and practicing the same skills at the same time. Sometimes the answer is "yes," especially when new skills are introduced or when a series of assignments is carefully sequenced. Other times, however, it may not be important to keep students all moving forward together in the same ways. If students will be doing group projects and presentations as well as written work, it is possible to schedule different sequences of activities for different groups of students. While some of the students collaborate, plan, and present, others might research, draft, and polish. There is clearly a tradeoff here: by juggling more complex lesson planning, teachers can gain a more steady flow of paper work.

While I know from experience that these strategies work, I suspect that the discussion of ways to manage student papers will continue as long as there are schools, students, and teachers. The problem is certainly not going to go away. In fact, the issue is especially compelling at present: the education system is under increasing pressure to meet assessment standards imposed from outside, and to do so with increasingly scarce funding. Class sizes are creeping upwards, despite research that tells us this is not a good idea. Experienced high school and college teachers are retiring, accepting early buyouts, or leaving the profession for other reasons. State testing programs drive curriculum in many areas. Mandated programs are underfunded or not funded at all by the states or the federal government. The workload for teachers is more likely to increase in the near future than to ease. Faced with these realities, and with the real need to teach our students to write well, we must keep devising and experimenting with ways to make the paper load manageable.

2 "Ungrading" Writing to Achieve Freedom for All

Jennifer D. Morrison
John Hanson Middle School, Waldorf, Maryland

I thought I had a heavy paper load teaching my regular and honors classes. I assigned students a minimum of two papers each quarter in addition to their regular homework and classwork. These papers required organization, correct mechanics, and intelligent content. Yeah, I had a lot of work to do . . . then I was initiated into the world of Advanced Placement (AP) Language and Composition. Students were writing a major paper per week, either planned or timed. Suddenly, I found I was buried under a mountain of written text, most of it analytical, requiring detailed instructive feedback and as much as twenty minutes per paper. For three classes totaling seventy-eight students, that came to twenty-six hours of grading for a single assignment. Lunch periods, evenings until 1:00 or 2:00 a.m., weekends, holidays, breaks, even bath times were engulfed in a sea of student work screaming for a grade, stealing every second of my time. And the chaotic crunch before report cards were due nearly broke me. I had to find ways to eliminate some of this insanity while still providing students with quality instruction and ample opportunities to write.

Enter the beauty of ungraded work. Like many other educators, I spent a long time believing everything had to be graded; otherwise students would not invest in the assignment. However, I soon found that when ungraded writing assignments were carefully designed, "[they gave] students writing practice and offer[ed] valuable feedback without the burden of heavy grading" (Center). In fact, as I grew to rely more on ungraded assignments, I found students wrote better, took more academic risks, and functioned on higher thinking levels.

Much of the research on ungraded work focuses on writing-to-learn strategies, which emphasize that writing is "more than an end product, a curricular goal in itself. Instead, . . . writing [is] the *means* to the end, as a way students can learn by exploring ideas and making connections between them" (Madigan, as cited in Klein and Aller). Such strategies as journal entries, quick writes, five-minute summaries, and reflective reactions dominate the literature on this topic (Britton; Fulwiler; Tomlinson). I found that I too began to use such low-prep methods of having students process information without adding substantially to my workload. Warm-ups usually asked students to write succinctly about a previous or upcoming topic. Journal entries were checked off for completion and discussed in small or whole-class groups. Exit slips or short reflections were stuck to my door with self-stick notes for fast feedback on the day's lesson. However, these typical writing-to-learn strategies, while helpful, were still not relieving the enormous amount of formal paperwork with which I still had to contend. I began to examine the biggest culprit—timed writings.

In preparation for the course-culminating AP exam, students completed multiple timed writings both in and out of class. These writings could quickly top fifteen to twenty assignments in a school year. Multiply that by the seventy-five to eighty-five students I had per year, and I was attempting to manage well over a thousand papers in timed writings alone. In talking with students about the timed writings, I soon discovered that many students feared the impact these unfamiliar writings would have on their grades. These student were the top performers—future valedictorians and salutatorians—who had learned to "play it safe" to protect their beloved GPAs. Taking risks and making changes were not popular ideas with them. Breaking out of their well-indoctrinated comfort zones was terrifying and risky. I needed to give them an opportunity to fail safely so they could practice writing and growing.

Armed with this knowledge, I began requiring students to finish all the timed writings, but gave them credit for the *completion* of the assignment and for putting forth effort, not for the actual product produced. Once a set of timed writings was completed (usually consisting of four to six exercises), students gathered their collection and the corresponding scoring guides for each assignment (usually provided by the College Board), and then individually, in pairs, or in small groups of three to four, they selected two pieces to submit to me for actual grades. I spent time at the beginning of the school year training them how to use a rubric to evaluate essays and to identify quality responses so that when the time came to evaluate their own work, they were equipped with the tools and knowledge to effectively do so.

Several benefits emerged from this process. First, by having to evaluate their own work before I did, students gained a better understanding of their own strengths and needs. They internalized the standardized scoring guide (the 1- to 9-point AP rubric), which better prepared them for future writings. They could confer with other students, collaborating and discussing the merits of each piece of writing. These dialogues reinforced the concepts of what makes good writing—stylistic maturity, depth of analysis, insight, strong voice, and an organizational plan. Students became responsible for internalizing "quality" writing because they now took ownership of their learning; they understood the expectations and they were invested in the choices they selected. Ultimately, the decision of what to turn in rested with each individual student. Second, because students were choosing their best work to submit for a grade, they felt they had the freedom to fail, to have a bad day, to try new styles of writing, and to break out of their tired (and safe) ways of writing. Their grades would not suffer; thus their enthusiasm and subsequent learning increased. Writing became, as stated by Richard Gebhardt, "a way to discover what to communicate, a means of clarifying ideas, organizing data, honing broad concepts into an effective thesis, and adjusting assertions in light of new information or disconforming evidence" rather than an intimidating task. Third, and best of all, my workload was cut in half or even to a third of what it had been. I now had a mere fraction of the formerly overwhelming stack to grade.

My next venture was to approach the creative nonfiction writing I required of students to encourage them to find their own distinct voices. Over the summer, students were assigned William Zinsser's *On Writing Well* to read. Wanting to revisit and use this reading experience throughout the year, I asked my students for ways to incorporate Zinsser's advice into our class to establish more personal and less analytical writing. I wanted to achieve a balance between "transactional" writing, which tends to be evaluative, and "expressive" writing, which is "'close to the self,' [. . .] relaxed and familiar rather than formal" (Britton et al., as cited in Danielson). We developed a scenario in which students chose one of the seven instructional chapters per quarter, reread the chapter, and then wrote an essay applying the strategies given in the book. The chapters included such topics as how to write about a place, a person, sports, art, or humor. This gave students flexibility because it allowed them to choose areas of interest or expertise, yet it also forced them to try new writing styles, formats, or topics they never would have tackled otherwise. For example, while Carlos was a champion cross-country runner, he never thought to write about how he felt while running until he was faced with this assignment.

To encourage a climate of risk-taking and experimentation, we decided to make the grade for the paper based solely on turning in a quality effort. The criteria for "quality effort" were established by the students. Students' essays could flop, but if they made genuine efforts and demonstrated professionalism in their submissions, they received full credit. Because I was asking for risk-taking and trying to provide a safety net, I did not grade these papers on merit at all. In fact, unless the student requested it, I did not even put comments on the papers. The attempt at writing out of their comfort zones belonged solely to the individual students, and I only responded if they chose to include me. Often, they sought peers for feedback instead. This drastically reduced not only the amount of reading required of me, but also the level of scrutiny I had to apply, which can be very time-consuming. To reward those who felt they had done a particularly good job, we decided students could individually choose to have the paper reviewed for an additional grade included in their quarterly average. This grading plan validated their efforts by allowing them to receive credit for excellent work and gave them a chance to try something new without fear of their grades suffering. I could still provide students with valuable writing opportunities, but without overburdening my own workload. Additionally, since I was now reading fewer papers, of better quality, reading the assignments became enjoyable, reinvigorating my desire to teach and subsequently reenergizing the students to learn.

I have found this assignment to be consistently successful. In portfolio reflections written at the semester and end of the year, students often cite these papers as their favorites because they were not only purposeful, but also personal. They felt they had the freedom to explore ideas in writing they had not ever had the chance to do previously. From Corey's vivid descriptions of south of the border to Jean's critique of Henri de Toulouse-Lautrec's paintings to John's searing laments for a lost relationship, these papers strongly reflected students' memories, lives, and interests. Many students also commented that through these assignments, they better understood more traditional, stringent forms of writing. Jennifer claimed that through writing an ungraded memoir about her sister's birth, she "finally discovered how to organize [her] thoughts and was better able to write the required critical analyses of books afterwards."

As I have talked to other educators about my experiences with ungraded work, I am often met with the counterposition, "Yes, it might work for the AP classes; those students are motivated. But it wouldn't work with other classes." I have found this statement to be false. All students benefit from the chance to write without the risk of teacher judgment or requirements. Giving *all* students freedom to choose their writing and grading systems increases their level of confidence and subsequently improves the quality of their work. The fear of failure is removed. Matt was an often overlooked student with subaverage grades, but when he was allowed to choose what to write and what to submit for a grade, he soared. And because he viewed the sharing of his work as nonthreatening, it helped foster a stronger student-teacher bond. "I really need someone like you who cares [. . .] who goes out of there [sic] way for a troubled kid like me," he stated in a reflective response.

I view writing as an exploration and a journey to understanding. Student writing is a learning process. Perfection should not be sought; comprehension, insight, depth of understanding, stylistic maturity, and effort should be. Students should feel a sense of security in order for them to risk breaking out of the old, established patterns to truly write with passion and spirit. They cannot do this if they feel everything they write will be turned in and scrutinized or criticized. My goal is for students to feel as Maelina did when she discussed the growth she saw in her English portfolio. "I'm not afraid to write anymore. I learned it's okay to be a not so good writer; the only way to improve is to write. My fear of turning in a piece of writing is [now] gone." A key way to achieve this level of comfort is to use ungraded work and student self-selection. "Courses that regularly give students opportunities for ungraded, impromptu, low-stakes writing give them opportunities to re-phrase course content in their own words, to make tentative connections, to hypothesize, to inventory current knowledge, to make ultimately useful mistakes, and to articulate questions. Ungraded writing also relieves obsession with surface corrections. Students therefore begin to see writing as a tool they can use, rather than as just an occasion for numerous small failures" (Penn State). It is easy for us as educators to see ourselves as the persons responsible for evaluating all student work, but when we empower students to take ownership of the quality of their work and give them the tools to evaluate that quality, the learning becomes their own, and we are energized because of their successes and because we are not burdened with the paper load.

Works Cited

Britton, James N. *Language and Learning*. New York: Penguin, 1970.

Britton, J., T. Burgess, N. Martin, A. McLeod, and H. Rosen. *The Development of Writing Abilities (11–18)*. London: Macmillan, 1975.

Center for Teaching Excellence. University of Maryland. "Large Classes: A Teaching Guide [to] Writing in Lectures." 2004. 30 Jan. 2004 www.cte.umd.edu/library/large/writing.htm.

Danielson, Lana M. "The Improvement of Student Writing: What Research Says." *Journal of School Improvement* 1.1 (Spring 2000). 30 Jan. 2004 www.ncacasi.org/jsi/2000v1i1/improvement.

Emig, Janet. "Writing as a Mode of Learning." *College Composition and Communication* 28 (1977): 122–28.

Fulwiler, Toby. "Writing: An Act of Cognition." *Teaching Writing in All Disciplines*. Ed. C. Williams Griffin. New Directions for Teaching and Learning 12. San Francisco: Jossey, 1982. 15–26.

Gebhardt, Richard. "Writing-for-Teaching Idea Sheet #1: Low-Stress Ways to Stress Writing in Large Classes." 2002. 30 Jan. 2004 http://www.bgsu.edu/departments/english/rcweb/lstress.htm.

Klein, Bill, and Betsy M. Aller. "Writing Across the Curriculum in College Chemistry: A Practical Bibliography." *Language and Learning Across the Disciplines* 2.3 (Apr. 1998): 25–35. 30 Jan. 2004 wac.colostate.edu//llad/v2n3/klein.pdf.

Madigan, Chris. "Writing as a Means, Not an End." *Journal of College Science Teaching* 16 (1987): 245–49.

Tomlinson, Sandra. "Writing to Learn: Back to Another Basic." *The Changing Face of College Teaching*. Ed. Marilla D. Svinicki. New Directions for Teaching and Learning 42. San Francisco: Jossey, 1990. 31–39.

Writing Across the Curriculum Program. Penn State University. "Using Ungraded, Informal Writing-to-Think Exercises." 1998. 30 Jan. 2004 www.psu.edu/dept/cew/faculty/informal/htm.

Zinsser, William. *On Writing Well*. 5th ed. New York: Harper, 1994.

3 Grade Less, Teach More: Overcoming Student Resistance to Collaborative Paper Assignments

Allison Berg
James Madison College, Michigan State University

"I detest collaboration—I always end up doing all the work."
"Lindsay said she'd meet me at the library but I couldn't find her, so I wrote this paper on my own."
"Please don't assign a project like this again. It took forever and I honestly think it would've been easier to write it by myself."

Given students' low opinion of collaboration, even writing teachers who believe that composition is an inherently social process typically shy away from asking students to coauthor papers. Most prefer to let an initial "group brainstorm" or a final "peer edit" stand in for more sustained collaborative work. Perhaps a lack of experience with collaboration in our own scholarly lives—the vast majority of publications in the humanities are single-authored works—prepares us poorly to guide students through the intellectual challenges of coauthorship. Perhaps a reluctance to mediate potential student conflicts and logistical snafus, the simplest of which is captured in the second student comment above, discourages instructors from assigning papers that require a significant amount of student cooperation outside of class time. Certainly remarks like those of the first and third student send instructors a powerful message: students feel most comfortable, and are least likely to complain, if we require them to be responsible only to themselves.

Students' greater comfort with individual authorship stems, of course, from their encounters with a succession of teachers whose assignments and grading practices reinforce the idea that writing is fundamentally a solitary activity. Our collective failure to challenge this notion creates the single biggest obstacle to successful collaboration, a mutually reinforcing suspicion of coauthorship among teachers and students. "If collaboration were a 'normal' part of the writing process," one can imagine a first-year college student thinking, "why have I never had to do it before?" Meanwhile, an instructor might harbor doubts about whether coauthorship is either fair or effective: "Isn't it foolish to give two students the same grade for one paper without being certain that their contributions to it were roughly equal?" "Won't the better writers resent the weaker writers for holding them back?" "Won't the weaker writers miss an opportunity to learn more about their writing problems through individualized instructor commentary?"

Reasonable as these questions are, collaborative paper assignments have many advantages for both instructors and students that outweigh these pragmatic and philosophical concerns. The most obvious advantage for instructors is that requiring students to coauthor one paper out of the several typically assigned over the course of a semester cuts one's grading load for that particular paper in half (assuming students work as partners, which I advocate, rather than in larger groups). A less obvious but more important advantage is the extent to which a well-guided collaboration fosters individual students' self-reflection on the writing process.

What follows is a handout I provide for students in tandem with their collaborative paper assignment. It serves three functions: to explain my rationale for requiring collaboration, to prepare students for some of the logistical and interpersonal challenges of coauthorship, and to specify the questions they will need to answer in the final, individual reflection I ask them to submit with their collaborative paper. By providing these guidelines in advance, I hope to motivate students who take a negative view of collaboration to consider its possible advantages; to help all students avoid the most common roadblocks to successful coauthorship; and to indicate that the criteria for success on this project encompass more than the typical, product-oriented expectations for an individually authored paper. Of course the overall quality of a coauthored paper remains the most important factor in evaluation, but by asking students to submit written reflections on their experience as coauthors I have an opportunity to evaluate aspects of each student's engagement with the assignment, and with the collaborative process itself, that would otherwise be invisible in the paper. From students' point of view, the chance to submit a self-reflection makes the extra effort involved in collaboration "count" for something.

Why Collaborate?

Collaboration makes writing more social and potentially more fun.

Collaboration cuts down on procrastination and "writer's block."

Collaboration makes it more likely that you will come up with a strong argument (more original and more complex than you might come up with on your own).

Collaboration helps both writers develop their ideas more clearly and completely through a mutual feedback process.

Collaboration makes you aware of assumptions you bring to a topic and how others might see things differently.

Collaboration makes you aware of your own writing *process* (strengths and weaknesses) in contrast to your partner's. It also makes you more aware of your writing *style* (strengths and weaknesses) in contrast to your partner's.

Collaboration develops interpersonal skills essential to academic and workplace success (see "Tips," below).

Tips for a Successful Collaboration

Try to identify each other's strengths and use them to your advantage. For example, is one of you more of an "idea" person while the other is more of a "structure" person? Does one of you write drafts very quickly and easily, while the other struggles to produce a first draft but is skilled at revising or editing? Does one of you enjoy the research process more than the writing process, or vice versa?

Try to become aware of your "collaborative style," be up front with your partner about your tendencies, and agree to address any problematic areas. For example, if you tend to be a "pleaser," force yourself to be more assertive; if you know that you're a "control freak," make it a goal to be more open to the collaborative process. If you're a "safe" writer, make it a goal to take more risks; if you tend to be disorganized, force yourself to be more methodical in how you order your ideas.

Agree to tell each other honestly if you are unhappy with how the collaboration is going at any stage of the process. For example, if you think you are doing too much work, it's *your* responsibility to SAY SO. Or, if you think your partner is dominating the decision-making process, it's *your* responsibility to SAY SO.

Always, always, always show up when and where you say you will—on time!

Reflecting on Collaboration

Budget your time so your paper will be completed enough in advance of the deadline to allow each of you to type up an informal reflection on the collaborative process. Please address the following questions:

—To what extent (and how) does your paper reflect a successful collaborative process?

—To what extent (and how) does your paper reflect the limitations of collaboration?

—What did you learn about yourself (e.g., your strengths and weaknesses as a writer, a coauthor, or a team member) through this process?

—Which of your own contributions to the paper do you consider most successful?

—Which of your partner's contributions do you consider most successful?

—What, if anything, would you do differently next time?

—What two reasons would you add to my "why collaborate" list?

—What two pieces of advice would you give to future students faced with a collaborative writing project?

I deliberately skew my reflection questions to emphasize the positive aspects of collaboration. I ask, for example, which of their partners' contributions were most successful, not how their partners may have dropped the ball. I also stress to students orally that I will not mediate any interpersonal conflicts that might arise because learning to identify and address problems as they go along is one of the major, shared tasks of this assignment. At the same time, my reflection questions balance the expectation that they will have discovered two good reasons to collaborate that are not already on my list with the acknowledgment that they will probably also want to alert me to some of the "limitations of collaboration." Still, by phrasing my final question in terms of advice they would give to future students, I hope to turn any disgruntled students' attention away from what was frustrating about collaboration toward a consideration of what concrete strategies might have made the process work more smoothly.

What I hope students learn is that the process of collaboration, like the writing process itself, involves a series of problems that must be solved. The best student reflections show signs that collaboration has not only heightened a students' awareness of some of the perennial problems a writer faces (Where can I find relevant information? How should I organize my ideas? What is my most important point? How can I make it matter to my reader?) but also, by revealing another writer's composing process, given them a wider repertoire of strategies for solving them.

Of course, no matter how well I prepare students, and no matter how game most students are to try this novel approach to composition, collaboration *is* difficult. Rather than minimize this difficulty by asking students to collaborate on the most straightforward writing assignment in a given term, I generally require that they collaborate on a paper assignment complex enough to raise real writing problems. In doing so, I aim to encourage positive interdependence by making the collaborative paper assignment one for which two heads really will be better than one. For example, I frequently require a collaborative paper in the second semester of a yearlong writing course for first-year college students. In this particular course, which culminates in a substantial historical research project, students write four major papers: the first is a "Source Excavation Paper," an annotated bibliography of primary and secondary sources on a specific topic from the 1920s; the second is a "Primary Document Analysis Paper," in which students identify, interpret, and contextualize significant rhetorical features of a document unearthed as part of their source excavation project. The third and fourth are a formal research proposal on a 1920s topic and a ten-page research paper based on this proposal.

Because the annotated bibliography requires very little decision making in terms of format and organization, I have found that it provides too little impetus for real collaboration; it lends itself, instead, to dividing up the writing tasks and then cobbling together individually authored sections. The second assignment works much better, not only because it can be organized in any number of ways and requires students to discuss their differing interpretations, but also because it comes early in the term. Students are thus in a position to apply the insights gained through collaboration to their third and fourth papers. Moreover, knowing that they have two more opportunities to redeem a lower-than-hoped-for grade on the collaborative paper goes a long way toward preventing student resentment of a required collaboration.

An additional pedagogical advantage of assigning a coauthored paper is the effect coauthorship has on the peer-critique process. In my courses, students typically type up a formal critique of one other student's paper draft and discuss their comments with the student in the following class period. This method typically leads to a dyadic response model, because even if students share their critiques in peer groups of four or five, only one peer reviewer has detailed knowledge of each paper draft, and only one author is in a position to respond to the peer reviewer's suggestions. However, when two pairs of coauthors pair up for a four-way critique, each paper gets two separate peer reviews, without increasing the workload for each peer critic, who still writes just one critique. Moreover, in the subsequent class discussion, all four members of the peer group can discuss both drafts knowledgeably (having coauthored one and written a formal critique of the other), multiplying the possibilities for successful revision.

Although I have emphasized the troubleshooting strategies I use in assigning collaborative work, the majority of my students find collaboration a welcome break from the isolation that accompanies most of their writing projects. Some even ask if they can collaborate on their final paper project. For the instructor, the only drawback to requiring a self-reflection essay as a means to drive home the most meaningful lessons of collaboration is that some of the time saved by assigning a collaborative paper is used up reading students' self-reflections. Yet these responses are almost always enjoyable to read, frequently provide a springboard for discussion in subsequent conferences with individual writers, and rarely require written comments. They do, of course, demand additional work from students, who are right in concluding that writing a paper individually would be easier, but can usually be convinced that the insights gained from collaboration pay off over the long haul. If our goal as instructors is not only to reduce our grading load but also to enhance student learning, a "collaborative paper plus reflection" assignment represents a smart investment of our own and our students' time.

4 When Will You Stop Correcting Student Writing If You Don't Stop Now?

Ned B. Williams
Brigham Young University–Hawaii

This essay is for teachers who may wish to stop correcting student writing, but can't. That's right, stop, or at least reduce drastically the amount of time you devote to correcting student papers. Few of us hunger to edit student essays, and often students place little value upon our brilliant comments and our esoteric proofreading symbols, so why not stop correcting papers, or consider a few ways of facilitating revision tasks? Begin living the dual dream of every writing teacher: dramatic increases in the quality of student writing and delicious decreases in the time we spend editing their work. Instead of correcting fragments and semicolons and misplaced phrases and errors in logic and lamenting in the margins about the lack of evidence and writing lengthy critiques at the end of that tangled-up research paper, you could be reading books at Borders. Here are a few activities to try before buying your next red-ink pen:

Use post-up proofreading. Require all students to hand in assigned papers at the beginning of class. Promptly at the top of the hour collect all essays and tape or pin up each page of each paper on the walls in your classroom. Use the wall space of the entire room if you can. Once the students have settled into class, organize them into groups of two: one the reader, the second the marker. Invite these teams of two students to spread out around the classroom. Assign pairs to read aloud and correct at least four essays, and require them to write copious comments on each paper—you might display an example of the kinds of comments you expect. Pair the less gifted writer with the class genius. Don't worry for now about reading what students are writing on their classmates' essays. Just get them writing on one another's papers. Give prizes (I give out style guides and handbooks) for the most corrections per page. At the end of the hour, ask students to find their papers, review the comments, and bring a revised essay to class the following day. Facilitate the process but don't correct anything. Roam around the room as students work, join pairs, ask questions, compliment reviewers for writing good suggestions. Let students learn to revise by doing it in public under your guidance. But don't edit or correct papers at this stage.

Require evidence of five drafts of each paper before you accept it. These five simple words will transform the quality of any essay or research paper. Assign students to attach four preliminary drafts to the final draft as part of the draft package they hand in to you. Weeks before this assignment is due, I take ten minutes in class to show students how some papers evolve by displaying five discrete drafts of a single paper. The first draft can resemble brainstorming notes, mind mapping, power typing, speed writing—any essay-creation activity to give students a sense of discovery and creativity. The second draft is typed, proofed, and edited by the student. The third draft goes through the "post-up proofreading" process (see above) guided by a checklist tailored to the assignment. The fourth draft must have a signature from one of the tutors in your reading/writing center, if you have one. The final draft (number 5) comes in attached on top of the rest. This approach works very well for research papers. You will receive higher-quality student writing after you put the five-draft requirement in your next course outline.

Use a document-quality checklist: Many instructors use these from time to time with varying degrees of effectiveness. Here is where you transform your values regarding the quality of writing into a streamlined form, usually no more than a page. Give points for everything you expect from the student: breathtaking introductions, correct integration of quotations, sizzling diction. Whatever principles and characteristics you value highly in student writing belong in this checklist. I include one point for double-spacing the text, thirty-five if the quality and the amount of research fulfills the assignment. Include in this form your most common irritations, veiled in positive language accompanied by a fair number of points on the grading scale you may use. For example, instead of writing on future papers, "I am unable to see the link between these two paragraphs," simply have a question on the checklist that reads: "Have you put in **bold** font the sentence or phrase that connects each paragraph to the preceding one?" Great, two points. Let the checklist, when it can, nudge students toward writing that reflects your values. Instead of feeling like Bartleby the Scrivener each weekend facing stacks of unedited student papers, why not convert the features you advocate as a writing teacher into a practical, word-saving form, and get the students to fix their problems *before* you read their papers? When students are using a checklist tailored to your standards and preferences, you are no longer class editor-in-chief for each paper nor is your desk the place where unedited essays pile up. Rather, students are learning how to correct their own work, guided by a word-saving, ever-evolving checklist.

Make use of sixty-second peer review. At the beginning of the class, collect all assigned papers (yes, the five-draft package—see above). Immediately redistribute the papers in class and ask your students to read their classmates' essays, one paper per student. Ask them to read until they begin to lose interest in the content of the essay in hand. Ask them to draw a long line under that sentence or paragraph where interest wanes. Go through three to four iterations of this review step until several lines appear in each paper. Then return the papers to the author and say, "Notice where three of your classmates have indicated they are losing interest in your paper. Weak, perhaps, are your ideas, your sentences, your topic—something, who knows? Reread your writing and look for places where you can gain and regain the reader's attention. Change your essay so that your readers keep reading." Novelist John Gardner once told me and a small group of younger writers a few weeks before he died: "When your reader realizes he or she is reading, you've failed." The writer's mission, we tell students, is to deny each reader the chance to lose interest. OK, I realize how this activity, if handled poorly, might discourage some students. Also, a few student reviewers might not take the assignment seriously and draw a line in an arbitrary place just to signal their distaste for the paper or for the assignment. However, for a snapshot critique of the quality of the content of a paper, this activity works well, it goes quickly, and writers receive an immediate reaction to their writing—a line in ink or pencil with a message: electrify your prose, please. With few exceptions, the next version of each essay is markedly superior to the previous draft. Quality increases, and the time you devote to editing shrinks. And you aren't grinding your way through prematurely submitted student prose—they are.

Correct instances. All right, you are feeling mildly guilty about this teacher-free, hands-off approach to revision, and you feel you must write something on a student paper. After love or hate or the drive for survival, editing another person's paper is, quite candidly, the most powerful human desire known to most writing teachers. Instead of correcting the entire paper, consider restraint and correct only the first page. If errors abound, correct only those on the first page and return the paper with the following request: "Using the corrections on this page to guide you, correct all other such errors that may appear in the rest of your paper." If you have tutors in a reading/writing center on campus, require your student to meet with one and go over each sentence in the essay. Delegate revision; involve others. It takes a village to raise a writer.

If you want students to assume more responsibility for and feel more interest in their writing, then consider using one or more of the ideas above. Relinquish your role as the sole editor of student papers and return the responsibility to the students, where it belongs. So, when will you reduce significantly the time and effort you devote to correcting student writing? Why not now?

5 Assigning Writing in a Literature Survey Course: Applying WAC to English

Linda S. Bergmann
Purdue University

As a Writing Across the Curriculum director and consultant for many years, I have worked with faculty in many disciplines, helping them devise writing assignments that they could live with. I have always been sympathetic to faculty concerns about how to handle the paper load in large classes, because WAC initiatives can be quickly derailed when faculty find themselves swamped with work for which there is little reward. However, my own first experience with a large paper load took place only after I had been teaching for many years, mostly in relatively small writing classes—twenty-five students at the most, and often fewer in advanced, specialized courses. Then, as a member of a small department, I found myself teaching a survey of American literature, which usually drew fifty to sixty students, mostly nonmajors. Although this was not a writing course and there was a considerable body of material to be covered, I felt that I had to include writing as a central aspect of the course, both because I firmly believe that students should write in all classes, and because I could hardly maintain my credibility as a WAC director if I avoided assigning writing in my own courses.

Anticipating a sizable paper load for myself gave me the opportunity to put into practice some of the advice I have given my colleagues:

- Set clear goals for what you want students' writing to accomplish.
- Calculate how much time you have to teach students how to write and to respond to students' writing, both inside class and out, and consider carefully how that time might be best used.
- Make sure that the relationship between your goals and your time is realistic—and adapt your plans accordingly.

Goals and Limitations

Because students in this course were mostly nonmajors taking an "introduction" to literature that for most of them would also be their last course in the field, my goals for assigning writing were more limited than they would be for a different kind of class. One of my main goals for the course was that students should understand and enjoy literature enough to want to read it occasionally on their own, and my goals for their writing were similarly general. I wanted them to

- have the opportunity to do both informal and polished writing;
- demonstrate that they were keeping up with the reading and at least starting to comprehend it;
- generate questions in response to the reading that would be of genuine use in focusing the class, both to me as a teacher and to their peers;
- gain some experience analyzing literary texts; and
- learn some of the genre-knowledge for writing an English paper, and have a chance to produce a reasonably finished paper by revising a draft after receiving feedback.

Being realistic about my time constraints as a teacher and administrator, I considered four other factors as I designed the writing component of the course:

- I was able to give no more than two in-class hours to explaining writing assignments.
- I was able to give some—but limited—time outside of class to working with revisions (about ten hours).
- I could not commit to reading sixty-odd papers at a time, on the same topic, and certainly not to reading them twice, once for revision and once for grading.
- The course grades should be easy to calculate and my gradekeeping time should be kept to a minimum.

Given my goals and time constraints, I decided, in addition to giving three short-answer exams, to assign three different kinds of graded writing in the course: informal discussion questions, a short paper written in two drafts, and an optional informal argument justifying a grade for class participation. Our school had just adopted Blackboard, and I used its electronic gradesheet, class listserv, and small-group features to simplify communication and gradekeeping. I devised a 1,000-point scale for the grade sheet, distributed as follows:

Exam 1: 150 points (covers readings to date)

Exam 2: 150 points (covers readings since exam 1)

Final Exam: 250 points (covers entire course, with extra weight on readings since exam 2).

Paper (choose one of the six topic options): 250 points

Discussion questions (5 sets at 20 points each): 100 points

Class participation: 100 points

Discussion Questions

My purposes for assigning students to write discussion questions were (1) to provide an opportunity for them to engage in repeated, short, informal writing tasks; and, (2) to give me feedback on students' reading in time to use it in class. This assignment was an outgrowth of the "one-sentence paper" I had often suggested faculty assign at the end of each class—i.e., students write on file cards the most important thing they have learned in that class period and a question that remains to be answered. Many of my colleagues in engineering had tried—and liked— that approach to informal writing in large classes. However, when I tried it, I found myself baffled by the sheer number of responses and questions I received. I altered the assignment by requiring five or six students to submit questions before each class, and these proved to be a genuine help to me in shaping each class session. In addition, I could rely on at least five or six students having finished and thought about the reading before class (a real plus in a general education course).

I divided the course into three segments, separated by the exams, and required students to sign up for four question sets, at least one in each segment. After some tinkering over the semesters, here is a final shape for the discussion-question assignment:

> Discussion questions will be used to provoke class discussions of texts; they should point to controversies about how the text can be understood or interpreted, rather than merely asking for answers that are easily available in the readings. For example, instead of asking "Why does Benjamin Franklin think that it is impossible to eradicate pride?" ask a question like "How stringent is the moral code that Benjamin Franklin lays out in his book of thirteen virtues?"
>
> At the end of the first week of classes, you will sign up for the specific days on which your questions are due. Each set will consist of four questions, and must be submitted to me via e-mail by 9:00 a.m. on the day of the class. I will expect to use these questions to shape the discussion for the day, and I may send them to the entire class if that seems useful.

Grading: Appropriate sets of questions that are handed in on time will receive 20 points. Late questions are obviously useless, and will receive no credit.

Handling the paper load: There was no paper load from this assignment, and it was a genuine help to me in planning classes. The subject line for all questions was to be "discussion questions," so that I could easily sort each day's questions by subject and immediately enter students' credit into the electronic gradebook. I came to expect to use the questions in my final preparations for class, and often either forwarded particularly interesting questions to the entire class or read them in class to start a discussion or generate additional questions. Occasionally, I e-mailed a quick compliment to a student whose questions were particularly insightful or a suggestion to a student who submitted a noticeably weak set. The students seemed to enjoy the chance for input into the class and the occasional immediate feedback, and I appreciated knowing when they were confused and how they were responding to the material being covered. Grading, even with comments, took no more than five minutes before each class, and this assignment took almost no time to explain in class, since to provide models of excellent questions I merely forwarded the best questions to the class listserv.

The Short Paper

I knew that if I assigned a single paper I would have to grade a huge batch of papers on pretty much the same topic, and if it were due late in the semester, most of them would be hastily written and bear little trace of revision. By the end of the semester, few students would have the time to take advantage of using the writing center, even if I offered extra credit for it, and even if the writing center could handle sixty appointments at once. Moreover, I knew that although spending class time describing how to write a paper generally has little impact on students' performance, small-group work can be effective in helping students to see and meet expectations. Again, I couldn't possibly cram six or seven small-group meetings into one or two weeks. It occurred to me that there was no need to have all the papers due at the same time, and so I decided to offer students a choice of topics at the beginning of the semester, staggering the due dates for the papers. That allowed me to run a small-group workshop for each paper, at intervals of about two weeks, which I could more easily fit into my schedule. It also meant that I needed to grade ten or fewer papers on any one topic in any one week, a much brighter prospect for me than grading sixty at once, although perhaps some instructors prefer marathon sessions of paper grading.

The course calendar offered students a choice of writing a paper on one of six authors, due on the Friday of the week after we had finished reading and discussing that author's work in class. I chose the authors I was most familiar with—Benjamin Franklin (Week 4), Nathaniel Hawthorne (Week 7), Frederick Douglass (Week 10), Henry David Thoreau (Week 12), Herman Melville (Week 14), and Walt Whitman (Week 15)—and allowed no more than ten papers on any one author. The diversity of due dates gave the students some choice as to the genre and time period of the author they would write about, as well as the (much-appreciated) opportunity to fit the papers into their personal and academic schedules. They had two weeks to browse the anthology before making their choices, and were advised to work their choices around other major events in their lives (social events, religious holidays, and major tests or due dates in other courses). I required students to e-mail me first and second choices, but it turned out I was able to give each student his or her first choice.

I constructed a fairly detailed "master paper assignment" that laid out my expectations for the paper, into which I pasted author-specific topics a week or so before each paper was due, thus being able to shape the assignment according to the class discussions and to make further use of the questions students submitted before class. Although a greater lead time would be useful for more advanced students, for this class a week was sufficient for students to think about and write the three-to-four-page papers. I also customized a grading template I regularly use to fit this particular assignment.

The day before each paper was due, I held an eighty-minute workshop session in the writing center, which let me introduce one or two tutors at the end of each session. These workshops were optional, scheduled during a cross-campus free period. (If that period had not been available, I would have scheduled them in the evening.) Word soon got around that the workshop sessions were very useful, and the attendance level was high. Students were expected to come to the workshop with their first drafts, and most brought at least a partial draft. At the workshop, I spent about half an hour discussing how to use citations (always a big issue for these undergraduates) and the appropriate citation form for the text they were writing about, answering students' general questions about the paper, and discussing the grading template. Then I asked students to read their papers aloud until they came to their main point, a workshopping technique that has two advantages: reading their own papers aloud helps students hear whether they actually have stated a point and understand when it needs to be clarified; and listening to other students' papers helps students develop a broader sense of what can be argued and of how their classmates' readings of a text or issue may differ from their own. Finally, I introduced them to at least one of the writing tutors and invited them to make appointments for individual consultations. Usually appointments could be scheduled before the paper was due the next day, but when students could not fit an appointment into their schedules I granted an extension on the spot, with the paper due the weekday after the first possible appointment. Again, for a more advanced class, I would have offered more lead time, but most of these students wrote their first drafts on Wednesday, to bring to the Thursday workshops, and had no trouble rewriting them in time for Friday morning.

Handling the paper load: As I mentioned earlier, I find it much easier to grade six to ten papers at a time than to be faced with a pile of fifty to sixty, and so the paper grading seemed easier than expected. I graded the papers using my holistic template, which describes the qualities of letter grades, then transposed letter grades to numbers (using a point schedule) for the grade sheet. Distributing and discussing the grading template in advance made the grades seem meaningful to the students, which meant that I could write short comments on each paper that went beyond merely justifying the grade. Grading the papers, then, became a regular small task, not an onerous chore, and I was usually able to return them the class period after they had been submitted.

Even better, the quality of the papers was higher than I had expected. Since most of the students attended a workshop session, at which they had a chance to discuss questions about their papers with me as well as to hear their papers in the context of their classmates' work, they produced quite thoughtful and polished papers, with a strong sense of audience.

Informal Class Participation Argument

I like including a grade for class participation, since oral discussion is a good way for students to practice analyzing texts (one of my goals for the course), but I have trouble keeping track of it fairly and consistently, particularly for a large group. Therefore, early in the semester, I informed the students that they were responsible for keeping track of their own class participation, and that I would expect them to make a case for their grade in this area. As the semester progressed, I told students that I would give each of them 65 points out of 100 for class participation (a grade of D), and if they wanted a higher grade they could write an argument (no more than a page) that demonstrated why they deserved it.

Handling the paper load: Since Blackboard lets every student see his or her own total points, the "bookkeeping" was left to the students. Students who could see that their grades might be raised by an additional few points were happy to take this opportunity—but they were usually no more than a third of the class. These papers were easy and fun to read, and took little time to grade. Those students who bothered to make an argument usually made a strong case, in good spirit, documenting when they had participated and describing what they had learned in the class.

Concluding Observations

The key to making writing work in this course was in realistically considering how much time I could give it, and then carefully thinking about what use of that time would be most effective in reaching my goals. Two aspects of my planning helped keep the paper load under control. First, I arranged the course to minimize the time I spent on gradekeeping and other paperwork, so that the potential for me to respond to individual students was maximized. Second, by staggering the due dates and workshops across the semester, I was able to assign a paper, oversee revisions, and provide a genuine response to the students' efforts at writing—which would not have been possible in any other way.

The informal writing worked well because the discussion questions offered the opportunity for short but meaningful contact, repeated at intervals throughout the semester. The students could see that I actually read, responded to, and used their questions, and the questions encouraged a high degree of personal interaction between the students and me.

Finally, teaching this course left me grateful to have had the opportunity to practice what I had preached to my colleagues, and even more respectful of faculty across the disciplines who make an ongoing effort to assign and respond to students' writing.

6 Enhancing Learning and Lessening the Paper Load with Students' Portfolios

Rita Al-Abdullah, Ebru Erdem, Ellen K. Johnson, Duane Roen, Jennifer M. Santos, and Lauren Yena
Arizona State University

Although teachers readily understand how portfolios can enhance learning by encouraging students to be more reflective about their work in writing courses, the prospect of managing the volume of paper or electronic files in portfolios can seem daunting. The good news, though, is that students' portfolios need not increase the paper load or file load for writing teachers. The trick is to guide students so that they, not we, manage the bulk of the paper load.

Beginning with Learning Goals or Outcomes

Before we describe strategies for keeping the workload manageable for teachers, we want to make the case that portfolios are most effective in enhancing learning when students construct them to demonstrate learning against some set of goals or outcomes. In first-year writing courses, for instance, many college programs have asked teachers to use the Council of Writing Program Administrators' "Outcomes Statement for First-Year Composition," which includes four major areas of skill sets and knowledge: (1) rhetorical knowledge; (2) critical thinking, reading, and writing; (3) processes; and (4) knowledge of conventions. By referring to these outcomes throughout the course, students will be prepared to address these issues effectively in their portfolio-analysis assignment.

The Portfolio Assignment

Teachers in programs that have adopted/adapted WPA's Outcomes Statement typically will give students a portfolio assignment that might include the following language:

> As you construct your portfolio this semester, your task is to re-
> flect on what you have learned in the four areas of WPA's Out-
> comes Statement. To that end, please write a cover letter that
> makes the following kind of assertion: "Here's what I have learned
> about writing this semester." As you support that assertion in the
> cover letter, you will need to draw on the wide range of work
> that you do throughout the semester—drafts and revised versions
> of formal papers, notes on peer-review sessions, journal entries,
> reading notes, and any other artifacts that illustrate your work.
> Although you may sometimes need to support a specific asser-
> tion by quoting several paragraphs from a revised paper, at other
> times you might only need to include a single comment from a
> journal entry or a peer-review session.
>   I am giving you this assignment on the first day of the course
> because I want you to begin constructing your portfolio now.
> Throughout the course, you will have opportunities to reflect on
> your work in various ways.
>   Although you may prefer to submit a portfolio in print form,
> I encourage you to construct an electronic portfolio because that
> will mean that you, your peers, and I will have less paper to lug
> around. You may decide to construct a word-processed file with
> hyperlinks to the evidence supporting your assertions about what
> you have learned. Alternatively, you may decide to construct a
> Web site with appropriate links to supporting documents.

Students' initial responses to a semester-long project can be varied. For many, assessment of isolated learning aims has been the norm,
and an extended exercise such as this may make them apprehensive
about completing the project successfully. Therefore, clarifying course
learning outcomes helps students to see that their portfolios represent
more than a massive accumulation of coursework. In addition, the outcomes provide them with a set of criteria to consult as they appraise
their work.

Begin the portfolio-assessment project by brainstorming ideas
together about the kinds of questions students might pose for each of
the objectives. Evaluating rhetorical knowledge might include giving
examples of strategies, evidence, and voice used in their writing. Critical reading, writing, and thinking goals are measured when students
identify the strengths and weaknesses of each paper and explain how
tailoring arguments according to purpose helps them with projects outside the composition classroom. It is helpful to provide examples and
to discuss how peer evaluations, teacher comments, and multiple drafts
aid their final essays. Such examples and discussions demonstrate how
students can consider process goals while also considering their progress
in matters of style and standard writing conventions.

Examples of Heuristic Questions

To illustrate the kinds of questions students can use to discuss their emerging portfolios, we draw again on the WPA Outcomes Statement. For its specific categories, students might consider the following kinds of questions:

1. Rhetorical Knowledge
   - What are some purposes for your writing in this course? How have you fulfilled those purposes?
   - What have you done in your writing this semester to meet the needs of specific audiences?

2. Critical Thinking, Reading, and Writing
   - How have you integrated your thinking with the thinking of others in any of your writing projects in the course?
   - How have you used writing as a tool for learning this semester?

3. Processes
   - What kinds of composing processes have you used this semester? How have you adapted them for various writing projects?
   - How have you used peers to critique your writing in this course?

4. Knowledge of Conventions
   - What have you learned about documenting sources this semester?
   - What kinds of surface features have you learned to use with more confidence this semester?

Building Portfolios throughout the Semester

Encourage students to develop a plan early in the semester for organizing materials they may use in their portfolios. Whether you teach online, in a computer-mediated classroom, or in a traditional setting, briefly discuss options and the rationale for using different storage containers, such as disks or the university server to store drafts, media files, and scanned documents, which might include class handouts and handwritten notes. Providing a list of campus information-technology resources will lessen the anxiety level for technology novices, allowing you to spend your time helping students with composition issues. Also, consider how you might gather, assess, and return student work in a way that coordinates with their organizational plans.

If you are teaching a hybrid or computer-mediated course, students can download all their process work and final drafts for individual paper assignments onto a floppy disk and turn it in for assessment, keeping the workload manageable for both the teacher and the student. Advise students at the beginning of the semester to organize their disks by labeling each file clearly and by saving files into the corresponding folders on the disk, making it easier for them to review their work at the end of the semester and for teachers to view the files and insert their comments using the editing features in whatever word-processing program they are using. After returning their work, students can then make the necessary revisions on the same file, which helps lessen the paper load. The same process can also be used during peer-review sessions by having students exchange disks.

Reading Students' Portfolios

Reading students' course portfolios need not be an onerous task. An effective strategy here is to assume that you may only need to read the cover letter that a student writes. If the student's assertions in the cover letter correspond to the student's work that you have seen throughout the semester, you might choose to look at very little of the supporting evidence provided. Our experience has been that teachers may need to read some supporting evidence, but it is rare that a teacher needs to read great quantities of it. Further, if students construct electronic portfolios, clicking hyperlinks to supporting evidence is relatively quick and easy.

Although an obvious point, reading and assessing student portfolios (whether electronic or print-based) can be accomplished more quickly when tightly focused, well-organized work is submitted. To this end, we ask students to write reflections on both their processes and their products for each major writing assignment. Further, teachers can provide opportunities for more frequent reflective responses by presenting prompts for journal entries at an earlier point in a paper cycle. Such prompts encourage students to discourse on:

- aspects of their draft(s) that instill feelings of pride;
- issues with which they are struggling (including specific problems and strategies for resolution);
- strategies they are currently using to complete the assignment and how well those strategies are working;
- how their process differs from the processes they employed in previous writing assignments (in this course or other courses); and

- how the strategies and/or topic could contribute to coursework outside of the composition classroom.

Regularly fulfilling such tasks provides students with more than just practice for the more formal portfolio analysis assignment. It also gives them encouragement to produce a body of critical and reflective materials that can be used to construct the portfolio-analysis assignment. This type of regular reflective emphasis helps ensure student success and likewise encourages the building blocks of clear, concise prose that relieves pressure on the teacher.

Trends in Portfolios

Increasingly, students are encouraged to submit electronic portfolios, and the coupling of the online writing classroom with electronic portfolios unites the best of both. Electronic portfolios reinforce the online classroom experience by providing further interaction with technology. They also offer opportunities for individualizing: students choose the technological tools they will employ in constructing their portfolios. The potential for developing multimedia artifacts depends on the interests and sophistication of the user. Photographs, video clips, animation, and sound might be incorporated into their artifacts, allowing students with a flair for technology to experiment creatively while the less technologically oriented students can also creatively enhance their skills by using technology at their level of competence. Cultural literacy is stimulated at all skill levels in constructing the electronic portfolio. Technology stimulates critical thinking as students practice self-directed learning, making independent decisions about technology use, time management, goal setting, and the self-assessment that compiling a portfolio requires.

Webfolios are electronic portfolios that reinforce the concept of audience through online publishing. Collaboration occurs as student and faculty easily access the student's work. A free flow of ideas and skills can enhance students' learning and stimulate the integration of technology with their academic experiences.

Constructing capstone portfolios in writing classes may be important training for another trend: some universities now require students to compile a portfolio representing their accomplishments over the span of their college careers. This type of portfolio has the advantage of demonstrating students' development over time, providing a collection of their significant academic experiences and evidence of academic accomplishments. Portfolios may be linked to projects. The trend is to provide a demonstration of students' experience, knowledge, and skills through projects and the portfolio. Some consider the documentation of the scope and quality of students' educational experience that portfolios and projects provide to be a more equitable method of evaluation than traditional testing.

Teachers' Roles

Trends in evaluating portfolios reflect flexibility. One approach values the process of constructing the portfolio by evaluating students' individual projects only after the portfolio has been compiled. If writing is a process, it is reasonable to encourage student writers to develop their skills. In ESL classes where the teacher-as-facilitator is important to fostering student confidence and trust in the writing process, portfolios are not evaluated by the classroom teacher but by two other teachers or by a committee. If a classroom teacher does not agree with the evaluation, the mechanism exists to discuss the evaluation. This system's goal is to combine the teacher and the facilitator while adhering to standards of literacy.

Benefits of Portfolios versus Other Forms of Assessment for Students

By foregrounding and explaining specific, detailed course outcomes from the first day of the semester, portfolios can help to reduce the confusing ambiguity about how student writing will be evaluated—a confusion that students have repeatedly expressed. As the demographic makeup of student populations continues to diversify, students bring increasingly different preparations and expectations to writing courses. With learners hailing from very different educational and cultural backgrounds, there is an even greater need for establishing clear course goals. Making the criteria for evaluation visible and explicit for students is one way to address this issue.

Unlike standardized tests and other forms of assessment that have tended to treat writing as a decontextualized skill, portfolios also facilitate more situated assessments of writing within the context of larger, evolving projects. They promote consideration of revision processes, crucial activities that timed writing exercises by definition cannot allow. As a result, portfolios may encourage students who have struggled with these other forms of assessment to let go of reductive senses of themselves as generally "deficient" writers lacking skills and to adopt a more dynamic view of themselves as learners engaged in complex processes. Because learning objectives, such as those in the WPA Outcomes Statement, describe detailed knowledge and skill sets in four major areas, students can identify with greater specificity and accuracy those aspects of writing that they have already mastered, and those areas in which they might benefit from more focused practice and instruction.

Whether the finished documents themselves are print-based or hypertext, the activity of portfolio construction and analysis resonates with the critical and textual analysis that is a subgoal of many writing program curricula. Perhaps more important, when students are primarily responsible for collecting, organizing, and reflecting on their work, they may attain a greater sense of ownership for their own learning. Although teachers will assess the portfolios at the end of the semester, this process as we have described it asks students to engage in the kind of regular reflective and evaluative activity that has traditionally fallen on teachers' shoulders. Such activities encourage the self-reflection that sustains lifelong learning, a larger goal of any learner-centered education.

Work Cited

Council of Writing Program Administrators. "Outcomes Statement for First-Year Composition." *Writing Program Administration* 23.1/2 (1999): 59–66. 10 Nov. 2004 http://www.ilstu.edu/~ddhesse/wpa/positions/outcomes.htm.

7 Writing as a Process of Discovery

John A. Poole
Hobbs Middle School, Shelley, Idaho

Writing is a process of discovery, of finding out who we are, what we believe, and how we sound on paper. Students, especially, explore their identities and their voices through writing. Tom Romano, in his book *Clearing the Way*, states, "In any writing class, then, the first and constant order of business is to enable all students to establish and develop their own voices" (6). Because writing is a process of student self-discovery, grading every piece of student writing can thwart that effort. Romano underscores this sentiment, stating, "Be sure to cut students loose. Let them write rapidly and frequently [. . .] without regard to error, expectation, or self. Let them and you find out what they sound like when they know their words will not be marked wrong" (7–8). Allowing students to write without correction, while seeking to improve writing skills, may seem like an oxymoron. However, a portfolio writing assignment can relieve the burden of constant teacher grading and editing, while giving students a chance to explore their identities and voices.

A portfolio writing assignment can be designed and used to fit the needs of all classroom writers, whether they are beginning, advanced, or somewhere in between. The writing assignments can be geared toward self-discovery, idea exploration, information synthesis, or any other conceivable purpose. The variety of writing assignments will meet the needs of all writers within the classroom, while allowing all students to explore various writing types.

I begin each school year with an explanation of what constitutes a portfolio writing assignment. I show them art portfolios as an example. I then read to them a quotation from *Leaving a Trace*, by Alexandra Johnson:

> Thoreau tore off birch bark as he walked around Walden Pond, jotting down ideas with pencils he'd made himself. Novelist Ron Carlson once stored scraps of paper in an old bag, now in computer files. One diarist I know finally got going by razoring out the few pages he'd managed to keep in a series of abandoned

journals, transcribing them onto his computer. After a stroke, May
Sarton was forced to dictate into a tape recorder. (36)

I allow them to choose their own types of writing portfolios because
the portfolios should reflect their personalities as writers. I want my
students to recognize that their writing portfolios can take any form they
desire, as long as it makes sense to them.

We then discuss the mechanics of how the assignment should be
completed. I begin with the list below. This list is by no means exhaus-
tive. I assign students a portfolio writing assignment every two weeks.
However, I give them extra points for writing in their notebooks whenever they feel inspired. Among NCTE's publications is a book by David
Powell entitled *What Can I Write About?* that can act as a resource for
writing topics.

Students have written on many more topics than those listed below. For instance, one senior student wondered what people would remember about him after he left high school. He turned this assignment
into a personal obituary. Another student was adept at video production. He wrote a script for an episode of *Masterpiece Theater.* He then
produced and filmed the episode for the class. The possibilities are end-
less.

Creative Choices

- Write a short story that includes plot, characters, and a theme.
- Write a play of at least one act.
- Write six poems (of at least eight stanzas each) or a longer poem
  of 120-plus lines.
- Generate a one-way conversation, either real or imagined.
- Write two book or movie reviews that could appear in the school
  newspaper (three-quarters of a page each).
- Summarize the contents of a book you have read.
- Write the lyrics to two songs, complete with choruses.
- Write a fable (see *Aesop's Fables*).
- Write a children's book that has a moral (ten pages minimum).
- Write a letter to your favorite movie, sports, or television star.
  Then mail it.
- Use personification to define a word, action, or feeling.
- Write an essay explaining your beliefs.
- Write up the script for a talk show like *Oprah* or *Rosie*—no *Jerry
  Springer.*

Essay Choices

- Recall a vivid childhood memory.
- Recall an accident or another incident to which you were an eyewitness.
- Write a description of a character in a book you have read. Describe him or her in such a way that the reader can get a mental picture of your character.
- Write an essay comparing the good and bad aspects of an issue.
- Present your position on an issue.
- Speculate upon the causes and/or effects of a problem or condition.
- Write a short story, based on a memory you have.
- Write a creative essay describing the reason you were not able to turn in a specific assignment.
- Write a letter to the editor of no more than four hundred words. Then submit it to the local newspaper for publication.
- Write a satirical essay.
- Propose a solution to a problem facing your community or school.
- Team up with a member of the class to develop a report on a topic in which both of you are interested.
- Analyze a novel you have read.
- Analyze a poem you have either written or read.
- Write a letter of application for a job.
- Write an argumentative paper.
- Explain a process.
- Write a report based on an interview you have conducted.

Most people are sensitive about the writing they do. This is especially true of students. They are afraid to have their writing examined because it might make them look "stupid." Johnson explains this as follows: "The Censor. It's that tight muscle of perfectionism. That dark, icy whisper. That confidence thief" (46). Students fear writing because they know that sometime, somewhere, I will grade their writing. Students lose sight of themselves in the attempt to write for me. Therefore, I try to make the writing process as nonthreatening as possible. I simply read each portfolio writing assignment, without taking the time to edit each and every error. I give each student's piece of writing a cursory evaluation, regardless of whether the piece of writing is polished or rough. I make a general distinction (for feedback purposes) by using the check system. √+ (great piece of writing) or √ (average piece of writing). This gives the students general feedback about their writing, without assigning them a grade. It also takes relatively little time. This evaluation allows each student to have my general impression of the piece of writing, without assigning a grade or making corrections. This quick evaluation allows the students to remain in control of their writing.

Writing evaluation is a thorny issue, but I tie this portfolio writing assignment to specific grammar principles and the Six Traits writing model. For each portfolio writing assignment there is a specific focus. For instance, the first portfolio assignment focuses on developing a great idea for a paper and developing effective essay introductions. As the students are composing their writing, they focus on these two issues. The next portfolio writing assignment incorporates organization and effective conclusions. This scaffolding process gives them a chance to build on previous principles and increase students' writing ability at the same time.

Once the students have written two assignments, we form evaluation groups. I mix the writers in each group and try to include a higher-level writer, an average writer, and a lower-level writer in each group. These groups are responsible for reading the writing assignment, focusing on the specific writing and grammar skills. Using the Six Traits writing rubric, they evaluate one another's writing. We focus on only one trait each time we evaluate. This keeps the students focused, but creates an effective foundation to move on to other writing skills. Then, at the end of each evaluation session, one student (selected by the group) from each evaluation group will read his or her writing aloud to the class. Evaluation groups take place after each portfolio writing assignment. Evaluating and sharing allows students access to a wide range of writing and ideas. These evaluation groups also allow students a chance to share their writing in a less threatening way than sharing in front of the entire class.

At the end of each semester, after careful evaluation, a student will type up one of these portfolio writing assignments into a final, polished copy. This copy should be (and usually is) one of the best pieces of writing a student has done. We publish these in a classroom book. I have found that when students see themselves published, they gain increased confidence in their writing ability, feel more motivated to write, and understand more clearly the purpose and value of their writing.

This portfolio writing assignment has benefited many of my students. Sarah[1] stated, "Looking back, my favorite thing was to do those portfolios. I know that we all complained about them, but it was so great to be able to write about whatever was on my mind. I think that it was what really made me love to write." Another student, Raoul, had seen his friend involved in an accident at a dangerous intersection close to our school. He wrote a letter to the editor to address this issue. As a result, our city council and school board found a solution to this problem, potentially saving student lives. His letter to the editor showed his connection with his voice and the purpose of his writing.

> Dear Editor:
> Yesterday, during lunch a tragedy struck our community. A young student of Hillcrest High School was returning from lunch. Upon stopping at the intersection of Sunnyside and Hitt, he waited patiently for the steady flow of traffic down Sunnyside. Seeing a small break, and already thirty seconds late for class this young man ventured out into the intersection. The car he was driving stalled in the intersection, and an oncoming motorist driving a large SUV struck him on the driver's side of his car. The car proved no match for the large 4 x 4 and the teenager was pronounced dead at the scene. Now amongst the splattered fry sauce and lemonade that smother the tattered Buick's dash, lie the remains of a young man's future, dripping just as grossly as the fry sauce. Once he had a promising future, several scholarships were being given to him. Now a black hearse offers a compromise for his future plans. Fortunately, this tragic event has yet to occur, but due to decisions by the city of Idaho Falls, and the District 93 school board, we might as well say that this tragedy will occur tomorrow, not "someday." The answers to this problem are simple and cost effective. Yet the city and my school board have adopted an unwritten policy of "let's lose a life first." Right now, an alternate exit from Hillcrest High School is barricaded. This exit would allow traffic to flow out behind Edwards Cinema, where it would then disperse at the traffic light on Hitt. Right now the city could install a much-needed traffic light at Sunnyside and Hitt, giving traffic on Hitt a fair chance to pass Sunnyside. But right now our city and my school board do nothing to solve the problem. How much do obituaries cost in advance? I would like to buy mine today.

The beauty of this type of assignment is that students direct their own writing. They are developing their own writing topics, developing and practicing editing skills, and working toward creating a publishable paper. Students can identify and explore their identity, explore various types of writing, and, ultimately, develop their voices as writers. Writing becomes, then, the vehicle that leads these students on a journey of discovery and expression. The teacher becomes merely the road signs on the journey giving direction to struggling writers. We, as teachers, can allow our students the freedom to develop their writing skills and ultimately sound their "barbaric yawp over the roofs of the world" (Whitman 96).

Note

1. Names have been changed.

Works Cited

Johnson, Alexandra. *Leaving a Trace: On Keeping a Journal; The Art of Transforming a Life into Stories.* New York: Little, 2001.

Powell, David. *What Can I Write About? Seven Thousand Topics for High School Students.* 2nd ed. Urbana, IL: NCTE, 2002.

Romano, Tom. *Clearing the Way: Working with Teenage Writers.* New York: Heinemann, 1987.

Whitman, Walt. *Leaves of Grass.* 1855. New York: NAL, 1962.

II Ideas for Engaging Students in Peer Review

8 "Everything Looks Great!" Revitalizing Peer Response by Taking It Out of Class

Hillory Oakes
St. Lawrence University

If in-class peer response is one of writing instructors' most common pedagogical tools, disappointment in the outcome of peer response may be one of our most common complaints.[1] Teachers ask students to read and comment on one another's papers with the best of intentions: we want them to learn to write and revise with an audience in mind, to realize that readers other than their instructors are interested and engaged in what they have to say. We may also look at peer reviewing as a way to reinforce concepts of style, grammar, argument, and organization taught in the course—a sort of self-policing among students. We expect that the feedback from a peer will help student writers see their writing through the eyes of someone else "on their level" and thus inspire them to rethink and revise their work in an invigorated way that mere comments from us instructors might not. In turn, instructors suppose (assume, hope) that the essays we receive from students who have done peer response will reflect this thoughtful revision and not look almost exactly like the rough drafts students brought to class for peer response in the first place.

Why, then, do final drafts and rough drafts sometimes look dishearteningly similar? Why does peer response often *not* invigorate students' writing and revision? Why don't students seem engaged in conversation with their peers about their work? And why do students appear surprised at the comments and grades given by instructors to writing that a classmate had already approved with "Looks fine"? In-class peer response fails in many cases because it takes place *in class:* students work in pairs or small groups, assigned to read silently a complete essay in a short period of time and offer immediate feedback—feedback that is often as silent as the reading and scribbled in response to a few teacher-prescribed questions. The in-class peer-response model is not conducive to learning or discussing revision; it is not even representative of a real act of reading, reflecting on, and responding to a piece of writing. Feedback from peer readers *is* important; students *should* learn to write to, read, and listen to each other, but how can we engage them in such critical conversations effectively?

For several years now, I have made peer response in my classroom much more engaging and productive for writer, reader, and instructor alike by moving the bulk of the peer-response work outside of the classroom. I ask students to take their peers' essays home with them, write response letters, and then hold conferences with their peers at the next class meeting. Students write serious, thoughtful responses for their classmates, who in turn find that their peer responders' comments provoke them to make more than superficial revisions. I would like to offer more detail about this method, which has proven increasingly successful for my students, as well as showing examples of my suggested guidelines for response letters and some actual students' comments. First, though, I want to summarize the problems of in-class peer reviewing as it is most commonly conducted.

Most of us have seen how a typical in-class peer-response session runs. Students bring copies of their rough drafts to class with them. The instructor lets students know what kinds of questions or issues they should focus on; the teacher may have a peer-response form for students to fill out as they go. In pairs or small groups, students exchange drafts and begin reading. Some may mark on the draft in front of them as they read; others may wait until they're finished to fill out the peer-response sheet, if one is available, or make notes. When readers are done, they return the drafts and their written comments to the writers; depending on the teacher's directions (and on the available time), they may or may not discuss their comments out loud. In some cases, students work in small groups and thus must begin reading a second essay when they are finished reviewing the first one.

This model of in-class peer response can go wrong at almost every step. One or more students may not bring a draft to class, even if required, so at least a few students at a time may be left idle, with nothing to read and respond to. At other times students may feel desperately pressed for time, especially if they are asked to look at more than one paper during the peer-review session. Teachers may give response criteria that are either too vague—"Tell the writer which places work and which don't"—or too detailed for the allotted time, which can be cut short by an instructor's explanation of the many questions on the peer-review sheet. And these peer-review sheets given for in-class guidance may hinder, rather than help, the exchange of constructive suggestions and feedback, especially if students do not have much space to write or much time in class to discuss their written responses with one another. Rather, students often get scribbled-on drafts, perhaps with a peer-response sheet, to stuff in their bags as they dash out of class.

When they come back to these responses as they revise their essays, their experience may be close to this hypothetical example:

> After returning to your dorm room from class, you excitedly remove three peer-response worksheets from your binder. As you begin reading your classmates' thoughts on your term paper, you see only a few comments: *"Thesis:* Sounds great! *Material incorporated from class:* Nice job using discussions!" Finally, one more side note: "I fixed a lot of your commas; maybe you should just double-check the grammatical mistakes." A feeling of relief settles over you with the realization that the paper is virtually finished. (Maddie Rappoli)

With this kind of minimal response to work with, students too often do assume that their papers are "virtually finished"; they make suggested surface-level changes ("just double-check the grammatical mistakes"), figuring perhaps that if any larger problems existed in their writing, their peer reviewer would have noticed.

The quality and quantity of the students' in-class responses suffer—causing students' revision and writing to suffer as a result—because in-class peer review is a highly artificial reading situation. Most of us would never dream of trying to both read and write out thoughtful comments on a student's five- to ten-page paper in a matter of fifteen or twenty minutes; in fact, some teachers I know won't even hold a pen in hand when first reading an essay so that they are not tempted to interrupt the flow of the reading process with circling and scrawling. Not all of us would want to comment on or grade a paper while the student writer caught what we wrote in her peripheral vision, nor would many of us choose to respond or grade at an uncomfortably small desk in a room full of people. Why should students require less amenable reading and responding conditions than we do?

Even the best student readers and responders in a class may feel rushed by time constraints, especially since peer review is rarely given an entire class period. Some students concentrate best in a familiar study space and can be easily distracted or discomfited by pages turning or pencils scratching; others are slower readers than their classmates, so when they notice some in the room are already finished, they may feel pressure to skim the paper in front of them and hurriedly write a few comments. Peer pressure can also affect the quality of the comments, as a student may feel reluctant to make detailed criticisms on a paper while the writer sits at his or her elbow. Moreover, the social pressure of the classroom can lead to mixed signals: students may take what time they have to write constructive comments but tell their peers out loud, "It was fine. I really liked it," potentially deflating the effect of the suggestions for revisions they wrote down. And even when students have time and comfort to articulate their comments, too often these comments tend toward proofreading and overlook or gloss over concerns with thesis, organization, or development.

In the end, both students and teachers can end up exasperated by the process and outcome of in-class peer response. Certainly not all in-class peer-review sessions are fruitless, but I am sure that we have all seen (many times) something like the worst-case scenario I described above. If we want a better outcome, in which student readers have time to read, reflect, and respond and student writers get useful feedback from someone other than us, then all instructors should consider making peer response an activity that takes place, primarily, outside of class time.

My peer-response method in composition and literature courses is similar to what creative writers know as a workshop. Students in a fiction workshop, for example, are never asked to read and comment on a classmate's story cold but instead exchange copies well in advance of a class meeting so that they may read the story at least once and write up substantial comments to give to the writer at workshop. Along those same lines, I ask students to bring a printed copy of their rough drafts[2] to class on an assigned day (typically a Friday), with peer responses due at the next class meeting (usually a Monday). Students work in pairs—sometimes randomly assigned, sometimes matched by me—and will remain with the same peer-response partner throughout the course.

On the day students bring rough drafts to exchange, I instigate the process by asking students to write a short "memo" on the back of their drafts[3]; in this memo they outline the major concerns they have about their drafts (thesis, use of clichés, and "flow" are common) and list any questions they have for their readers ("Do you understand how much time has passed between the first two sections?" or "Can you help me figure out where I need more evidence?" for example). Then I allow them five to ten minutes to meet with their response partners, explain what their papers are about, and verbalize some of the concerns and questions in their memos. Afterward, the class and I go over peer-response guidelines that I draw up for each assignment (see the guidelines for a personal narrative and an academic paper at the end of this essay). The guidelines sheets ask many more questions than a typical in-class peer-response sheet might, but I make sure students know that they are not required to answer each and every one; instead, I intend the guidelines to help them focus their comments and, perhaps, to lend them terminology ("voice," "integration") that they might otherwise have felt reluctant to use.

Students then take their peers' essays and the response guidelines home and, as I schedule it, usually have an entire weekend during which they can take as much time as they need to read and respond. Using the guidelines sheet if they choose, students write a one-and-a-half- to two-page[4] letter addressed directly to the writers, detailing their reactions to the essays and their suggestions for revision; they are also free to mark on the drafts to point out problematic words, phrases, or passages. They are expected to bring two copies of the letter to our next class: one to return to the writer, and one to submit to me for credit.

With no limitation on the time they can spend reading or the number of comments they can offer, my students write response letters that, first of all, explain their reactions as readers, an important kind of feedback that is too often elided during in-class sessions for lack of time or lack of pertinent questions on a response sheet. Here is the opening to a response letter written by one student in my 200-level Expository Writing course:

> I think your essay was well-written and easy to follow. I really liked it because I could feel the emotion that you were trying to express, the times when there was tension and the times when there was happiness. A few times while reading, I had to stop because of the sadness. I liked the manner in which you developed the story because you based everything on a short timeframe; however, there was not much overlap of the events surrounding that period, and I had difficulty figuring out where some scenes were happening because the story seemed to move suddenly from the funeral back to the house. (Wanja Nyoro)

Wanja's explanation of her reaction as a reader offers the writer positive feedback ("I could feel the emotion that you were trying to express"); constructive criticism ("I had difficulty figuring out where some scenes were happening"); and an implied question about whether the emotional content was overdone ("A few times while reading, I had to stop because of the sadness"). Such comments would likely not fit easily into a box on an in-class response sheet, nor would they be fully conveyed in the shorthand of conversation taking place after in-class response ("I liked it," "It was good"). Wanja's response letter does something else that an in-class response might not be able to do: develop and explain an apparent contradiction. Though Wanja begins by saying, "I think your essay was [. . .] easy to follow," she later comments, "I had difficulty figuring out where some scenes were happening." The length of the peer-response letter gives Wanja an opportunity to reconcile these reactions as, near the end of her letter, she offers a constructive suggestion: "I mentioned earlier some inconsistency in your story. This actually goes away as the essay progresses, so consider going back to the parts I marked and making sure we know exactly where the events take place."

In their response letters, students not only describe their reactions as readers but also examine how the essays fit the assignment and the concepts we've been discussing in class. While during in-class response students may get to circle problem areas but not offer too many suggestions for fixing them, in peer-response letters they can explain both problems and potential solutions in more detail:

> I thought that the evidence you used was very strong throughout the piece, but [. . .] you know so much about [Christopher Marlowe's] mysterious death that you don't need to make this piece just a review of what others have already written. I wonder if you could use the emotional pull of death and mystery more. For example, maybe you could open the piece with a detailed scene of what you envision his death was like. Have your opening be this mysterious death, then develop your theories about this man and what surrounded such an interesting figure. Just an idea. (Amy Barr)

Students continually offer one another these "just an idea"s for revision:

> You told me the introduction needed some work, but I think it is not that bad. I like the imagery you give the reader, but maybe the first sentence or two don't have much to do with what your story is about. I think if you started off with a memory about the place, your introduction would do an excellent job of preparing the reader while not giving too much away. (Amy Neidlinger)

> So what are you suggesting? It sounds like you're saying college athletics should be eradicated altogether for the good of academics. Strange argument for a hockey player to make! I think you could make your argument clearer if you develop stronger connections between the social and economic factors that caused the rise in funding for athletics. You do a good job of illustrating how athletic departments cause a financial drain, but you haven't explained why or offered a solution yet. (Brenna Ferry)

Even comments about sentence-level concerns are more fully explained in the context of a letter, rather than circled mysteriously during an in-class session and called, vaguely, "grammar":

> One of your word choices confused me: "person-centered student body." What is "person-centered"? There were some overly repeated words, such as "busy" on page 5. Were these repetitions for effect or could you find a different way to say it? (Kendall Landers)

> Although your thoughts progress logically, your long sentences in this section make me lose the train of thought. Try breaking some of the long sentences up with semicolons so that each individual point is emphasized. (Adam Yagelski)

Comments as detailed as these are the norm, and students rarely have trouble finding enough to write about in their response letters.

When students return to the next class meeting, I allot approximately twenty minutes for them to meet with their partners and exchange response letters. During the same amount of time that in-class peer response sometimes takes for the entire response process, my students are instead able to continue in person the conversations they've already begun by reading and writing about each other's work. Students see the response letters not as a checking-off of boxes, not as proofreading, but as a true engagement with the other person's work that carries beyond simply doing the assigned response; I often overhear something along the lines of "I won't repeat everything I wrote in the letter right now, but let me tell you about some other things that came to me later." Students write down notes as their responders talk through the essays with them; then each member of the class takes his or her peer's letter home to help with revision. (I collect a second copy of the letter to read over and record for credit.)

A final test of the effectiveness of out-of-class response comes in the "critical preface" each student must turn in with the final, revised essay. This preface is a short reflective piece (one page or so) in which students explain how they decided on their topic, how they developed their ideas, and how they revised, including discussion of which of their peers' comments they used (or didn't use) and why (or why not):

> After I read all of my peer revisions, I went back and changed a lot. I took Brenna's suggestions on where to expand (the section on alternative grading systems especially), though she made one suggestion I didn't take (to discuss my personal history with grades). (Amy Barr)

> My peer responder's comments prompted me to think about my observations on a different level, such as the implications of my

idea of what would happen if students focused more on the natural surroundings. (Jaime Lyon)

For the most part, students seem pleased with the amount of commentary they receive from their peers and find peer-response letters to be a vital part of their revision process, as one student expressed in the preface to her final portfolio:

> Throughout the semester critiques from my peers have been indispensable. Through the eyes of others, I have learned to spot the flaws in my writing. Before, I didn't know what to look for; now I do. Also, criticism from others has helped me to improve my work, showing me where I need more information, what I could do to make any piece an easier read, and where the reader needs help or gets confused. Some of the revisions in this portfolio paper include providing an eye-catching header, providing my own opinion, and filling in some minor holes, all of which were suggested by my peer readers and which I probably wouldn't have realized I needed on my own. (Brenna Ferry)

As an instructor, I also find the peer-revision process vital. While I read and make comments on every rough draft my students write, I am as curious as they are as to what other readers might see that I have not. I find that they take their peers' suggestions seriously and are more eager to revise than they might be if they had minimal in-class response; it is as if they are afraid of letting their peer responders down. I am certain that I see more growth between rough and final drafts than I did when I practiced in-class response.

The time I invest in and out of class for my part in the peer-response process is probably about the same as it would be if I were still conducting peer response during class time: with a ten-minute meeting for "memos" and exchange, and another twenty minutes for peer discussion of comments and letters, I am devoting a total of about one-half of a class period to the endeavor—just as I used to set aside half an hour for in-class peer response. Since I take up a copy of each peer-response letter for credit, I must take some time on my own to read through the letters. However, I do not write comments on these letters (unless I spot a student struggling to offer adequate feedback), and the letter assignment substitutes for another short writing assignment that I might otherwise have asked for in its place. In fact, I believe that despite the time I must give students in class to meet with each other and the time I spend reviewing their responses, in some small way this out-of-class peer-response process saves me pedagogical energy. I see that students are learning together, and I see their writing improve.

Notes

1. I am indebted to Maddie Rappoli, a student in my Responding to Writing course at St. Lawrence University, for inspiring this title and providing the student's point of view on peer response included in this text. I also would like to acknowledge and thank other students whose writing I quote in this essay: Amy Barr, Brenna Ferry, Kendall Landers, Jaime Lyon, Amy Neidlinger, Wanja Nyoro, and Adam Yagelski.

2. Increasingly, I allow (and even encourage) students to e-mail drafts to each other.

3. If students are exchanging drafts by e-mail, I ask them to write the memo in the body of the e-mail message to which they are attaching their document.

4. This is a suggested minimum length; letters sometimes run three or four pages.

PEER-RESPONSE GUIDELINES: PERSONAL ESSAY

As you write your response to your classmate's personal essay, you may want to ask of it the same questions you'd ask of any personal narrative you read:

INTRODUCTION

- How does the introduction grab your attention (or fail to)?
- *Does the introduction intrigue without divulging everything?*

THESIS

- What is the message/theme/central image of the paper?
- *Is this message/theme/image implicit or explicit?*
- Does the message/theme/image play out well throughout the paper?

VOICE/TONE

- Is the essay in the first person? The third person? Does it shift between points of view? If so, is this effective or distracting?
- Is the essay told in present or past tense? If past tense, is all action and commentary in the past, or is the "present" voice making comments about past events? Is the choice of tense effective?
- What is the tone of the essay—humorous, nostalgic, distanced, serious, a combination?
- Are the voice, tense, and tone a good fit with the subject matter?

DETAILS/DEVELOPMENT
- What kinds of details (specific incidents, sensory descriptions, etc.) does the essay include?
- How effective are these details in developing a theme or idea throughout the essay?
- Are there strong transitions/connections between the parts of the essay?
- Are the incidents and details focused and specific enough for the length and purpose of the assignment?

STYLE
- Does the writer make clear and effective word choices? Does the writer avoid clichés and repetitiveness?
- How are the sentences structured? Is there a variety of sentence lengths and rhythms?
- What is the diction of the essay—that is, is the language formal (and if so, is it *too* formal or stiff)? is it informal (and if so, is it *too* informal or slangy)? Does it include certain specialized terms, and, if so, are they explained by the context in which they appear?

CONCLUSION
- Does the essay end abruptly or does it come full circle?
- Are all points brought up in the essay resolved in some way?

In your peer-response paper, write one and a half to two pages in which you answer some (but by no means all) of these questions as a reader. Compliment the writer on things he or she does well, but also constructively point out any areas about which you feel unsure. Make your constructive criticism (as well as your compliments) specific, and offer alternatives or suggestions when you can. You should feel free to mark on the paper itself, not only to point out such things as punctuation or spelling problems, but also to make suggestions or mark passages you refer to in your response. You should write the response in the form of a letter addressed to the writer. **Please bring TWO printed copies of the response paper to class on Monday.**

PEER-RESPONSE GUIDELINES: ACADEMIC ESSAY

INTRODUCTION
- Does the introduction get your attention quickly?
- Are the thesis and direction of the paper clear?
- Is there a "preview" of the main points the paper will explore?

THESIS

- What is the thesis of the essay? Does the thesis include a "because" clause?

- What kind of question is at issue? Is the thesis concerned with **fact, definition, value,** or **policy**? Does this seem to be the most effective way to look at the issue?

DEFINITION/HISTORY/BACKGROUND

- Does the writer define any key terms that may be misunderstood?

- Does the writer explain the background of the question at issue and/or give a brief outline of some of the events, discoveries, debates, or experiments that have led up to this question?

- **Does the essay seem to place itself in an academic "conversation"?**

EVIDENCE

- Does the writer support the argument with convincing evidence?

- Is logical evidence (quotations, statistics, facts, figures) tied clearly to the thesis? That is, is all cited information used to support the essay's argument, rather than just as padding?

- **Does the logical evidence come from reliable academic sources? Does the evidence come from more than just Web sites?**

- **Are all facts, statistics, quotations, or paraphrases of information from other sources cited parenthetically?**

- If emotional or ethical evidence is used (such as personal narrative or journalistic observations), does it integrate smoothly with the logical evidence?

- If the essay contains little or no emotional or ethical evidence, should it have more? If so, where would such evidence work well?

OPPOSITION

- Does the essay include fair acknowledgement of the opposing viewpoint?

- Is the opposition's viewpoint supported with some research, not just summarized in a perhaps biased way?

- Does the essay offer a convincing rebuttal of the opposition's argument?

STYLE

- Does the writer use comma, colons, and semicolons correctly?
- Does the writer **avoid the passive voice**?
- **Is the writer's language concise?**
- Is the writer's vocabulary not too informal but not too stuffy?

CONCLUSION

- Is the argument and the strongest evidence for it summarized one last time?
- Does the essay leave an opening for someone else to respond academically?

In your peer-response paper, write one and a half to two pages in which you answer some (but by no means all) of these questions as a reader. Compliment the writer on things he or she does well, but also constructively point out any areas about which you feel unsure. Make your constructive criticism (as well as your compliments) specific, and offer alternatives or suggestions when you can. You should feel free to mark on the paper itself, not only to point out such things as punctuation or spelling problems, but also to make suggestions or mark passages you refer to in your response. You should write the response in the form of a letter addressed to the writer. **Please bring TWO printed copies of the response paper to class on Monday.**

9 How I Conquered Peer Review

Barbara A. Mezeske
Hope College

The reasons for teaching writing as a process are myriad and familiar. So are the reasons for using peer review as part of that process. No one disputes the value of teaching students that the audience for their writing is broader than just the teacher, that their written voices are more authentic when they write for their peers, or that they can learn valuable lessons about writing by critiquing the work of others.

Like every other teacher who uses peer review, however, I have had my share of problems. During the first fifteen or so years of my college teaching career, I tried to solve them by a variety of creative and energetic strategies. I devised lots of specific, narrow questions for students to answer about their peers' work. ("Examine the introduction: does the writer succeed in arousing your interest? How?" "List three words or phrases that are examples of concrete language. If you don't find three, suggest ones that the writer might use.") I came up with questions that asked students to describe rather than to evaluate writing. ("In which paragraph do you find the writer's thesis? Restate it here." "Describe the organizational pattern of the middle of the essay.") On workshop days, I tried a range of different classroom strategies from simply passing each paper to three different readers, to having writers read aloud to a group of reviewers, to having groups of reviewers read *other* people's papers aloud. However, there was always something wrong. Weaker students gave poor feedback; better students felt cheated or used. At times, student readers changed or eliminated the very things that made a paper sophisticated or witty. Some students took the process seriously; others always had to be coached to offer more than one-word responses to peer-review questions. Peer reviewers' empty praise ("Good job!") set students up for disappointment when my grade was a C. Lacking confidence in their peers' judgment, some students insisted on my seeing their papers in draft form anyway. Others never took peer-review workshops seriously because it was only the teacher-read final draft that mattered to them. One semester I tried to control the review process by assigning a grade for the quality of the reviewers' responses. Another time, I tried assigning a grade to the drafts themselves. Both times, I doubled my own paperwork.

Frustrated, I asked myself what it was about peer review that was causing these problems. The answer was that the entire process lacked quality control. Certainly, some students followed instructions carefully and earnestly, and did good peer-review work. But in classes of twenty students, with everyone doing review work at once, I could never be sure who was working well and who needed more coaching to make the kinds of comments that were really helpful to writers. Moreover, students came into my classroom with uneven preparation for this kind of work: some were old hands at peer review and found my coaching excessive and intrusive; others had been trained in classrooms where "peer review" meant "check for spelling and mechanical errors," and they needed all the prompting and prodding I could give. Without vigilant oversight, the whole group threatened to sink to the lowest common denominator of response, on the principle that, if others were doing only superficial readings and critiques, why should anyone work very hard? Finally, I felt bad for the writers who really wanted to improve—every shallow or inadequate response made them less likely to value the entire process approach to writing.

The idea of peer review as part of the writing process was so important to me that I began to consider what I was willing to sacrifice in order to do it well. The answer, when it came, was simple: class time. Since I knew that I could improve the quality of peer review if I could participate in the review of each paper, I decided to do just that. I deliberately traded whole-class instruction time for small-group meetings devoted to peer review. The results have been gratifying.

Here's how it works. At the beginning of the semester, before I know any of my twenty first-year composition students, I divide them into five groups. The division is arbitrary, though I invite them to write the name of one person they would like in their group on a card. I take their wishes into account, though often students do not know anyone in the class. The workshop group stays together during the whole semester. Initially, I did this for my convenience, but I have learned that students develop supportive relationships with one another and like having a constant group. During the week that drafts are due, I cancel all regular meetings of my four-credit writing class. (That's four hours of class time at my college.) In place of those class sessions, I schedule four groups to meet with me for one hour each, and I meet the fifth group at a different, mutually agreed-upon hour. This means that, during the workshop week, each student comes to class for only one hour; I am there for five hours.

Each time a group meets we follow the same procedure. Students bring copies of their drafts for everyone in the group. One by one, they read their papers aloud while we all mark comments, corrections, and questions on our copies. When the reader is finished, we take a minute or two to finish writing at least one substantive comment. Then, each student listener offers the writer one oral comment. Because I am seated in their circle, I can prod to be sure comments are both specific and substantive. ("Which paragraph do you mean?" "What words, especially, did you have in mind?" "What do you mean when you say the introduction was good?") If students are at a loss for what to say, I draw their attention to specific elements of the paper. ("What do you notice about the sentence at the beginning of paragraph three?" "Do you think the final sentence is effective, or could it be dropped?") In effect, I am training students to be good peer reviewers. No one may repeat a comment that has already been offered. I am always the last person to comment.

During this process, writers are instructed to listen and make notes without engaging in discussion, although this is a difficult rule to follow. One of the most pleasant discoveries I have made using this method is that students *want* to engage in vigorous discussion of one another's papers! Also, students notice and are eager to point out how other group members' papers compare to their own. ("I could do an opening like Ashley's." "This paper has the same citation problems as the last one.") When everyone has had a turn, the students' marked-up copies of the draft are returned to the writer. However, I keep the draft copy in order to make more extensive comments.

This is the second significant change I have made to the peer-review process in my classroom. In addition to sacrificing whole-group instruction time, I have redistributed the majority of my own correction time to commenting on drafts rather than on final papers. This was not part of my original conception, but I began to do this almost immediately. I discovered that after listening to students read their own papers, and after participating in the group feedback, I had a really good grasp of the paper's strengths and weaknesses, and lots of clear suggestions for ways the writer could improve. It seemed only natural to communicate that to students right away, rather than wait until the final draft was finished. I left each hourlong session with four papers on which I could elaborate on the workshop comments, help students prioritize the sorts of revisions they needed to make, and suggest new directions. Because I was synthesizing my written responses from written and verbal comments I had already heard or made, I decided to word-process my responses. I gave them to students in hard copy, along with my copy of their draft, the next day. (See sample comment at the end of this article.) In my responses, I found it both useful and natural to refer extensively to comments already made by other students: this had the effect of validating the students' judgments and reinforcing the idea that peer review is worthwhile.

Final papers were always due a week after I returned my comments to the students. I generally succeeded in giving draft papers a one- or two-day turnaround. The final papers were submitted with all the marked draft copies and my word-processed comments. When I evaluated the papers, I began by reviewing my own comments and checking to see what the writers had done since the workshop. Because I had already heard the papers and had responded to them thoughtfully, I made very few additional comments. Evaluation went quickly.

Feeling smug about how well this system seemed to be working to alleviate *my* problems with peer review, I asked students to comment on our peer-editing practices as part of the regular student course evaluations. Feedback was very positive: "I like the groups." "Our group got along so well!" "It was worth it." I asked them to consider seriously whether they had been cheated of class time. After all, four peer-review sessions per semester meant twelve cancelled hours of class for each student. Responses were predictable ("I didn't mind not coming to class."), as well as thoughtful ("There was enough reading and library work to keep me busy." "I liked the independence."). Some responses were especially gratifying. ("At first I didn't take the group comments seriously, but I learned that they were important.") Even more interesting to me was the way the balance of the class shifted: the weeks during which we did peer review became the times that students looked forward to and talked about later. Workshop days were no longer dull, but were instead the most interesting and engaging part of the course. I attribute some of this to socialization, since many workshop groups bonded and became friends outside of class. However, in addition, the workshop hour was always intense and productive: we kept our eyes on the clock, avoided idle conversation, and stayed tightly focused on writing.

One other consequence of the sacrificed large-group sessions was that I relied on e-mail to stay in touch with the class and to provide instruction. For example, if the first workshop group had a lot of questions about using first- and second-person pronouns in their papers, I could fire off a minilesson via e-mail to the whole class. I assured them that they were responsible for e-mail messages as though they were lectures. I sometimes sent follow-up messages to workshop groups to clarify some issue they had raised about documentation, the library, or writing. I always used e-mail to tell the groups when I was finished with their drafts so that they could pick them up in my office as soon as possible. In this way, despite the loss of whole-group instruction time, I kept open the lines of communication between me and my students. This resulted in numerous one-on-one e-mail conversations about students' particular writing questions. Others who use this system might do even more work electronically, for example sending their draft comments to students by e-mail and having students submit final papers electronically.

Another effect of this system was to make whole-group class time more concentrated and focused. I tended to make longer reading assignments over the workshop weeks, and to require short, one-draft response papers that would kick-start discussion on the days we all met together. I gave students more independence to monitor their own time during the workshop weeks, and expected them to come to class the following week with something substantive. I used the e-mail conversations not only to monitor students' concerns about their drafts, but also to find out what other areas of the course were raising questions that could be addressed when we were all together.

Could this system be adapted to another setting? I think so, with some tweaking. The group size, for example, might be expanded to five or six, depending on the amount of time available and the length of the papers students write. Also, in high schools or other situations where teachers do not have the freedom to cancel classes, the teacher could participate in small-group peer workshops as long as the other students were meaningfully occupied. This might require some internal control apparatus such as a professional or student aide, or a carefully designed activity to occupy the non–group members. Students might be doing a reading assignment, using the library or computer lab, or working in groups on something else. If classroom management is a challenge, a teacher might participate in only a single round of group workshops in order to model good peer-review practice. Subsequently, he or she could revert to a whole-class workshop day, still using the same groups and the same procedures.

I have been using this system for seven years now. For the first time in my career, I am happy with the way peer-review sessions are running in my first-year writing classes. My students, despite varying abilities, are engaged and on task. I feel in control of a process that now works reliably. Perhaps most important, I have discovered how to invest my time in responding to student writing in a way that seems to make a difference in the way students write and think about writing.

Sample Response to Draft Paper 1

This paper begins with a good idea: to analyze a specific TV show and why it works. Thesis is in the right place, but may need rewording: it seems to place more emphasis on Bob Barker's role than you do in the paper itself.

Development: fleshing out connections between ideas. There are several places where you can examine your paper for this. Begin, however, between sentences 5 and 6 in the intro. What's this connection? How are you defining "reality TV"? What's the relationship between reality TV and ads?

I've been rethinking Heather's comment about your use of Fowles's article. Maybe she is right. You could add a phrase to introduce him: "Jib Fowles lists 'the need to escape' as one of advertising's fifteen basic appeals, and escapism is clearly one of the attractions of *TPIR*.. Like other ads which tantalize us with riches or luxury . . ." Do you think that would read better?

Also look at P5 (see below, too)—the sentence about Barker caring about the audience is not clearly related to neutering pets. But it could be—why does the audience care what he thinks about pets? Bc he seems to care about the contestants. (Give exs. of how you know this . . .)

Style: We love the specific references to the show—things that are said, what happens, etc. Concrete images make good, interesting writing. Sooo . . . add those product names, as we talked about in the workshop.

Clarity: P5's topic sentence. The sentence suggests that "program" is "ad," but what you mean is that a behavior is advertised, even though there is no sponsorship. This is a complicated idea. You might try, "One thing is advertised on the show consistently, even though no sponsor pays for merchandise or air time. Barker always concludes . . . "

- Missing "Works Cited" makes it hard to evaluate your internal citations. However, I hope we talked about citations enough, and that you can use Tara's (except for where she omitted the database she used) and Heather's for reference.

- Rewrite conclusion as discussed in workshop.

This was a good start—nicely specific, interesting to hear.

10 Conference Class Sessions: Reducing Paper Load While Supporting Student Revision through Effective In-Class Response

Karen Nilson D'Agostino
Brookdale Community College

Four of the five classes I teach each term at my community college are first-semester college-level composition classes and each class comprises twenty-one students. Having studied at graduate schools where the production of student texts was emphasized as critical to learning to write, I have long been committed to requiring multiple drafts of essays and numerous journals as an integral part of teaching composition. While employed full-time in this profession for just over twenty years, I have striven to continue to update my teaching to provide effective classroom instruction and help my students grow and learn as writers. However, all too frequently the results of my efforts in improving and refining instruction result in an increased number of student journals, practice pieces, and drafts of essays. And although I have been at this a long time, I still cannot, in good conscience, assign an essay, a journal, a draft, or a revision, and not read it and provide some form of response.

In community colleges there are no teaching assistants to lighten the load but there are approaches that can help. Responses to journals can be brief, using Peter Elbow–inspired underlines (double straight lines for notable words, phrases, and ideas and squiggly lines for those words or ideas or phrasing that are questionable) and an occasional "Nice!" or "Why?" in the margin. Final revisions of essays submitted for a grade (for which I use a rubric) can also be given brief responses. Yet a composition course does not comprise just journals and final essays, and thus cannot be taught using only words, phrases, and underlines.

The drafts of essays that shape students' growth as writers demand more extensive responses. This is especially true when we require students to use responses and comments to revise their essays: to revise, reshape, add, or delete and move their writing forward to more effectively meet the writer's goals and the reader's needs. Requiring more than one draft of an essay and providing responses to assist students in revision are important to our teaching and student learning. Acceptable revisions are more than edits; they provide evidence of improvement, as writers respond to peer and teacher feedback, attending carefully to the comments and suggestions provided.

For years I focused on teaching and guiding effective peer responses to shape the revision of student essays. Teaching students to respond effectively is daunting, yet I had them working in pairs and groups, large and small, reading essays and asking questions. However, after extensive peer-response sessions, students would stay after class, seeking my ideas for revision or guidance in assessing the peer responses. Clearly peer responses alone were not enough to help my students revise effectively. More feedback and response were required than the average first-year college student was able to provide. I decided that to teach and use peer response effectively, I would have to read not only the drafts but also the written peer responses. So I read the student drafts, highlighted effective peer comments, added my own suggestions and comments, and returned these drafts in the next class session for students to revise. The revisions seemed stronger, giving evidence that my highlighting and comments were helpful. However, the peer responses did not improve sufficiently during the term for me to abandon this extensive commenting practice. The paper load that resulted was overwhelming, with a new pile of papers waiting for response each night.

My colleagues and I commiserated over the volume of papers and responses when we talked in the halls and as we waited for the copy machine, and finally a few of us decided to focus our ideas and attention on examining the burdens and benefits of response and find a way to teach effectively without taking home a folder full of student essays from every class session. We talked about workshops, what constituted effective response, the nature and limitations of peer responses and teacher feedback, and finally, in very informal summer conversation, shaped a new approach: conference class sessions. A distinct variation on the traditional one-to-one conferences, conference class sessions would combine key elements that would meet our instructional goals, help our students grow as writers, and provide us with a lighter paper load.

Inspiration and Planning Better Routes to Response

Conference class sessions were inspired by the idea that "response *is* instruction" and "response time *is* instructional time." This rationale formed the foundation for our planning. Once we began to see response as instructional time, neither a teacher's homework nor solely the teacher's responsibility, we were able to find ways to include it more centrally as an element of instruction. It seemed reasonable to devote entire class sessions to response and response alone. Because students compose and revise three essays during the term, we decided to allocate three of fifteen classes as conference class sessions.

Instead of brief one-to-one conferences, we allocated half-hour blocks in which three students would meet with the teacher to discuss their completed first drafts and develop ideas for revision. These three-to-one sessions were designed to include teacher response for revision, engagement with students in the writing process, and peer reading and response. They were also structured so as to eliminate some of the mystery of teacher response from the isolated, unseen realm of home or office and bring it into the classroom. Moreover, this approach would allow us to teach as effectively as possible without reading and responding to student first drafts of essays, perhaps the most challenging and demanding of student drafts, outside of class time.

In developing and incorporating conference class sessions into my teaching, I worked to bring in the best of one-to-one conferences and eliminate some of the problems I had come across in traditional conferences. Instead of substituting ten-minute one-to-one conferences for class, I made the first important distinction for my students and myself: the conference class sessions were instructional class sessions. Class was not cancelled; it simply took another form, meeting with three students for a half hour at a time in our assigned classroom. Attendance was mandatory.

Our goals were to provide effective and appropriate responses, engage students in looking carefully at one another's papers, and enable the instructor to leave empty-handed, without drafts of student papers that needed responses. The conference class sessions have not only met these goals but have been readily embraced and valued by students as well. The logistics, which are detailed later in this paper, are carefully planned, so that expectations are clear and we are able to use conference time effectively.

In a course that requires three essays (and revisions of each essay) the conference class sessions were built into the weeks when a completed first draft would normally be due: weeks 4, 8, and 11. Borrowing one half-hour from an office hour allowed us to extend normal class hours and provide seven half-hour sessions to meet with a full class of twenty-one students.

The Nature and Elements of Conference Class Sessions

Class conference sessions are planned in advance each term with dates specified in the course syllabus. One week in advance, a chart with spaces for three names in each half-hour time slot is passed around the classroom and students select times for conference sessions. I post this information on a course Web page later in the week to which students can refer to confirm their times. Requirements for the sessions are explained in class: E-mailed copies of the essays are due at 1:00 a.m. on conference class days. This ensures that the work is completed, everyone has the same deadline, and ideally students have been able to get a few hours of sleep before the sessions. It also ensures that no one comes in empty-handed and there are no essays forgotten in printers or on disks at home.

Each student comes to the conference session with four copies of her or his completed first draft (or comes in a few minutes early to print extra copies). The first draft of the essays are planned and started in class the week before the conference class session, so the teacher has an awareness of topic choices as well as the intended direction that the essays may take. We begin with quick greetings and a brief reminder of the format, followed by an exchange of copies of essays and silent reading of all three. As we read, students are encouraged to annotate the copies of the essay drafts and to make notes in the margins to guide the discussion.

Students are encouraged to bring questions about their essays to the conferences, and when they do, we use these to open the conference session. Otherwise, I simply ask, "Where should we begin?" and wait for a response. We focus on one essay draft at a time and as we discuss each the students and I annotate our copies. As we begin, I initially do most of the talking, but as the conversations progress the sessions become more interactive. As with most thorough discussions about essays, we rely primarily on talk, with key words written in the margins of the essays to remind the student writers of the conversation. I often use a diagram, which I explain as I draw, to illustrate a point.

Setting a positive tone for student response is essential for conference class sessions. The purpose is to guide and motivate students to take the next step in revising their essays. It is important for the teacher to make a conscious effort to stay focused and cover the same essential elements for each essay: introduction, thesis sentence, effective transitions, etc. The advantage of working with three students at once is the availability of examples in any three essays under discussion. The groups are self-formed and the student writing varies somewhat, but there is something in every paper for us to point out as a strength. Essays that need transitions appear in the same conference sessions as essays that have effective transitions. Examples can be garnered from the drafts we read, yet the feedback for each writer is individual and focused on his or her writing and the next step: revision.

A secondary goal for conference class sessions is to guide and support meaningful peer responses. This practice was something I had gotten away from in my teaching because, despite my best efforts, I found that many—perhaps most—students were reluctant and uncertain responders. Using a student essay to model appropriate peer responses in class seemed to help the students whose essays were used as examples, but did not improve peer response overall. In a room of twenty-one students, few responded and far too many sat quietly with an essay in front of them, their thoughts and ideas elsewhere, waiting for someone else to comment. Despite my best attempts at scaffolding effective peer response, students seemed more focused on being kind rather than being helpful. The conference class sessions were designed to address this by encouraging student response.

The small-group structure and half-hour time allotted for conference sessions was designed to help raise the level of student engagement in reading, responding, and listening. In these small, focused groups with the teacher present, students have a responsibility to respond, and yet the size and nature of the sessions make this, in the words of one student, "less scary." Questions can be posed in a nonthreatening manner to help to build and develop student responses. Discussions of one essay can easily consume most of the conference time, so it is important to keep one eye on the clock, and allocate time equitably, if not equally, among the three student essays.

The opportunity for face-to-face response and reading drafts when students are present provides a wonderful chance to reinforce the concept of audience. The conference class sessions enable students to "see" how their essays are read by others as well as to demystify the nature of teacher response. They can watch teachers and students nod, laugh, or smile, or furrow their brows and reread parts of the essay that are unclear. The three essays also provide a range of specific examples and illustrations for each session. Whereas in a one-to-one conference a single point might be repeated in several sessions, in the conference class sessions one point can be made with three students at one time. Specific suggestions pointed out to one student are heard by three, thus adding to their understanding and knowledge about writing.

At the end of the sessions, all drafts are returned to the writers to use in preparing a revision, which is due at the next class meeting. I end each session as I begin, asking for questions and reiterating key points that I want students to bear in mind as they revise. The conference sessions feel more formative than evaluative. For the teacher, they eliminate the heavy load of reading student essays every week of the term, and they also effectively eliminate the teacher practice of procrastination. Students arrive at a selected time, and their essays cannot be put off. Each essay is read with the student present and the conference class sessions allow teachers to provide thoughtful responses face-to-face, where we can set the tone as supportive instead of judgmental and provide additional explanation as needed. Furthermore, a significant burden is shifted: from teacher leading students through revision with extensive written comments to teacher guiding students with verbal comments and requiring and allowing them to find their way.

At the end of the first conference class session, which lasted three and a half hours, I was exhausted. Yet I had met and spoken with each student, and they had all left with annotated copies of their drafts and an understanding of what was expected for their revisions. I felt confident that they could take those next steps independently as I left class without any student drafts, and, for the first time in a long career, went home joyfully empty-handed.

The next class session includes a follow-up on the conferences with a reflective journal written in response to the conference class session and revision. Revised essays are submitted for grades, along with the annotated conference session drafts. These are taken home and graded. The student journals attest to an overwhelmingly positive response to conference class sessions that recognizes the benefits of immediate feedback followed by an opportunity for revision. One student asked if every English teacher in the college taught this way and wondered aloud how students revise effectively without class conference sessions. That comment and the productive revisions of essays have convinced me that this approach can provide a balance in paper load and workload that works for students and teachers alike.

The chart in Table 10.1 makes some important distinctions between one-to-one conferences and conference class sessions and is followed by some specific logistical issues that have also shaped the conference class sessions.

Setting

Meeting in the classroom is important because it eliminates excuses for students' not attending because they cannot locate or have forgotten an office location. Additionally, the interruptions that plague offices and interfere with our concentration and attention (ringing phones, questions from students and colleagues) do not follow us to our classrooms. Space is also a factor, as three students do not fit comfortably into small offices. In a classroom designed for twenty-one students, there is ad-

Table 10.1

Elements	Traditional One-to-One Conferences	Conference Class Sessions	Improvements and Distinctions
Time	10 to 15 minutes	30 minutes	More instructional time within conferences. Students choose their conference times and can choose to work with friends or simply choose the best time for them as individuals.
Text	One essay	Three essays	Additional examples, opportunity to see peer drafts and glean ideas from more essays. More material covered in conferences.
Participants	Teacher and student	Three students and one teacher	More feedback, more than one point of view.
Setting	Office or classroom (usually office unless adjunct faculty)	Classroom (preferably with computers)	Holding conferences in classrooms provides a known location (in computer classrooms, technology access for individual follow-up, if desired, and printers for copies, as needed) suitable to adjuncts and full-time faculty.
Use of Technology	Not required for conferences	Schedules posted on Web page, essays e-mailed by fixed deadline	Students can independently confirm conference times; same deadline for all students (more equitable).

equate room for conferences, space for students to wait for their conferences to begin (instead of sitting in the hallway), and even computers for students to print essays or work quietly after their conferences. And although all faculty may not have offices, all faculty have classrooms.

Choices in Times and Groups

A piece of paper with time slots and three blanks in each half-hour is used for students to select conference times. Students who usually arrive early for class tend to choose the early conference times. Students sign up with friends or with those they sit near in class, so there is an informal support structure inherent in the groups. Scheduling conference class sessions during class time eliminates excuses for conflicting classes, sports practice, or lack of transportation. Students are scheduled to spend the entire morning or afternoon in class (our classes meet once a week for a three-hour class session) and the students believe they are getting the best part of this arrangement, an abbreviated class session three times during the term.

Conclusion

While there are still journals to read, practice pieces (short writings completed in class) to check, and final drafts of essays to grade, the load for me as a teacher is now lighter and more manageable, and the instruction for students is as good as I can provide. As we continue to teach using conference class sessions, we find that more colleagues are interested in applying this approach and that it is received with enthusiasm by those who have tried it. We expect this interest and enthusiasm to continue to spread.

11 Mountains into Molehills: Coping with Essay Overload

Patricia S. Williams
St. Mary Academy–Bay View, Riverside, Rhode Island

It is a truth universally acknowledged that a high school English teacher, novice or veteran, in possession of large mountains of essays to correct, comment upon, and grade must be in want of relief. My apologies to Jane Austen! As English teachers, we all believe that our students' development as effective writers requires that they write numerous essays. Out of our conscientious belief that good teachers should closely read and comment in detail on each essay, we create Matterhorns of paperwork. As an Advanced Placement English teacher, I have been creating and attempting to climb these mountains for years. This year, for the first time in my career, I have discovered a strategy that has made this "mountain climbing" not only easier but much more enjoyable.

As we began our Advanced Placement Literary Analysis course this year, my students and I explored representative examples of literature from various literary genres, analyzing and discussing in seminar fashion why these pieces "worked." In addition, we used Nancy Dean's wonderful workbook, *Voice Lessons*. This resource contains one hundred very short exercises in identifying how diction, syntax, imagery, and detail individually convey tone in short passages from well-known literary works. As a preparation for the essay component in the AP exam, these exercises are specific, relevant . . . and short. Assessing and grading these brief exercises took minimal time and produced the same result as any number of long essays. As the course proceeded, I began to realize that the students in my class were learning just as well from this strategy as they had from much longer assignments in past years. Not only that, but my workload was considerably more manageable. I discovered that I could focus more closely on each student's work and give it much more specific attention. Consequently, I was less stressed and more satisfied with my own assessments and my students were ready sooner to tackle the Advanced Placement–style essay and considerably more confident.

In the second semester we began to examine the three essays included in each of the five sample tests contained in our Advanced Placement preparation book. Ten of these essay prompts require the student to "show how the author (narrator, speaker) uses the resources of language to convey (express, demonstrate) his or her feelings (attitude, tone)" relative to the subject. The other five essays require the students to use the resources of language themselves to respond effectively to an open-ended question about some theme of a literary work.

For their first effort, the students wrote a forty-minute timed essay in class in response to the first prompt in the preparation book. We then discussed their work as a class in general terms—decoding the question, exploring various approaches toward fulfilling the requirements of the prompt, and analyzing the resources of language involved. Most important, we critiqued the essays using the rubrics provided at the front of their preparation book. These rubrics are organized according to the numerical grades that the AP exam readers use to evaluate student responses to the essay section. Through this strategy, the students were learning to self-evaluate.

Having practiced and assessed their work as a class, they were now ready for a peer-editing experience. For the next essay in the preparation book, students wrote rough draft responses at home, giving themselves only forty minutes. They then printed two copies of the *unrevised* essays and brought them to class. I collected one copy of each for myself and a classmate received the other. The essays were distributed randomly. For about one-half hour, each student critiqued a classmate's essay according to the AP exam readers' rubrics and then assigned a numeral from the grading chart in the AP preparation book to the essay and proceeded to write a one-page justification for the numeral chosen. In organizing this critique, students used their understanding of the question itself, the lessons learned in identifying elements of language, and their own writing experience from the first semester. All critical comments had to be substantiated. Meanwhile, I critiqued my copies of the essays and assigned my numeral to each rough draft according to the rubrics the students were using. When the students had finished writing their observations, I collected the essays and critiques and returned them to the appropriate student authors. We then compared my grades with the grade assigned by classmates. Amazingly, twelve out of the twenty students had assigned numerals identical to mine. Of the remaining eight, six had come within one numeral of my own score. The work of the first semester had been successful because not only had my students learned to recognize good writing but they had also internalized the lessons and were incorporating them into their own work. Students then discussed the comments on their critiques and I added my own observations. I began to think I might just see the top of the proverbial mountain.

I repeated this exercise on a regular basis. When the students had written, critiqued, and discussed the three essays in the first sample test in their preparation books, I directed them to choose *one*, revise it, and submit it for a grade. The graded revision, complete with my comments, the original rough drafts, and the student critiques were added to their portfolios. As each set of three essays from the preparations book was completed, students note in writing the weaknesses they need to address and the writing strengths they are beginning to develop. These self-generated progress reports will also be added to their portfolios to be referred to before beginning each new essay. With each essay, they will add to this chart thus giving themselves and me an overview of their writing status.

Not only has this approach sharpened my students' writing skills, but I have also accomplished my task as teacher without the mountain of paperwork that before loomed as large as the Matterhorn. I can focus much better on five essays per student than on fifteen, track student progress more efficiently, actually get a decent night's sleep, and occasionally chat with my family without making a prior appointment. My students and I now work as a team to evaluate and improve their writing. While my students and I accomplish as much as always in terms of skills and types of writing, I have experienced great relief in a task that I found often exhausting and counter-productive—the grading of mountains of essays. As a bonus, students love the teamwork and are motivated by positive peer pressure. They also share a much clearer understanding of how to write effectively.

I developed this strategy specifically for my Advanced Placement students and will certainly track its success through the AP scores achieved in May by this particular class. However, I now plan to extend this method to all of my other classes. I am excited about adapting the Advanced Placement rubrics across the board; certainly a more consistent rubric can only be an advantage to student and teacher alike. For me, this method has transformed the onerous task of essay grading. The mountains of the past are turning into molehills.

12 Using Peer Review for Improving Writing without Increasing Teachers' Workloads

**Lauren Yena, Jennifer M. Santos, Duane Roen,
Ellen K. Johnson, Ebru Erdem, and Rita Al-Abdullah**
Arizona State University

In this chapter, we offer a sequence of activities for students to use in responding to their peers' writing over the course of composing a full essay. The sequence is intended to illustrate a fairly comprehensive set of activities for a writing project that takes three to four weeks to compose, but teachers may wish to pick and choose only a few of the activities. We begin by offering suggestions for how to establish the peer-review groups, and move on to discuss how role-playing activities may help to structure group activities. Because teachers using course-management systems such as Blackboard may ask students to conduct some of these activities online, we also describe possible online adaptations. After explaining the sequence of activities in detail, we also provide some time-management tips for both students and teachers.

Setting Up the Peer-Review Groups

Assigning three to four students to each peer-review group provides writers with enough readers to offer multiple perspectives without overwhelming any particular group. If time permits, it may be useful to conduct an inventory of students' writing strengths and weaknesses before forming these groups, considering their individual needs and interests before matching them with peers. In an online or partly online course, this inventory could include gauging students' familiarity with technology, because it can be useful to have at least one member who is competent in using the course software and at least one member who is a confident writer. Instructors may ask students to compose techno-literacy autobiographies as an initial diagnostic assignment, requiring them to post responses to a prompt such as this one to a course discussion board:

> Compose a brief technoliteracy autobiography describing your experiences with computers and writing. Share your experiences with and attitudes toward (1) writing, (2) computers, and (3) writing with computers. What types of writing courses have you taken before? How did they use technology? How have you approached revision in the past? Because these autobiographies will be public, they will provide an opportunity for us to introduce ourselves and get to know each other.

Such an exercise provides students new to the technology with a relatively nonthreatening, low-stakes introduction to the course software, and familiarizes them with the process of posting their work online. One alternative to the autobiography assignment that also helps teachers identify students' strengths and weaknesses before placing them into peer-review groups is to design and distribute a survey that targets these issues—a feature also available through course-management systems such as Blackboard. After the groups have been formed, members may choose original group names that they will readily recognize on the discussion board or in class. Although these initial measures may seem time-consuming and cannot guarantee a foolproof combination of personalities, thoughtfully constructing groups at the start of the semester and then maintaining them throughout the remainder of the term can help to foster productive peer collaboration.

Role-Playing Options in Peer Review

There are multiple methods of approaching peer-review prompts. The most common one occurs in the form of questions posed by the teacher for students to address on a given aspect of the assignment. Alternately, students may be asked to respond to their peers' work with less formal direction. This approach invites students to apply their knowledge of the rhetorical context of the assignment as well as the concepts of a given unit in a practical way. Yet this approach can be daunting to students inexperienced with the process.

To enhance their confidence, we propose that students gain more agency over their comments and critical exploration through role-playing. In a three-person group, the author presents his or her work both orally and in written form. Other students respond to the work from the following perspectives:

- *believer/encourager*—points out and justifies strengths of ideas presented

- *doubter/devil's advocate*—responds critically by questioning such aspects, from the appropriateness of the scope and effectiveness of the topic to the relevance of supporting points

In a four-person group, the following additional role is suggested:

- *identifier*—compares the work to the assignment sheet, showing which parts fit certain requirements and which requirements are not yet addressed. For a formal argument, this person may spend time identifying ethos, logos, pathos, conditions of rebuttal, etc.

As the papers approach completion, the identifier's role may be switched to that of *synthesizer*. Essentially adopting the role of the author, this person engages in conversation with the believer and the doubter while the actual author remains silent, taking notes on the discussion and thus learning about points that must be clarified or addressed for effective communication.

Rotating the roles of the group members for each paper reviewed encourages the students to think critically from different angles and provides them with competencies to bring to their own work in the future. This approach also helps reinforce effective reading strategies that serve as a springboard into more effective writing practices that can be implemented in a face-to-face classroom, a virtual chat, or an electronic discussion board.

Combining Online and Classroom Peer Reviews

The greatest challenge in providing a stimulating and beneficial peer-review experience is fostering students' awareness of their ability to review and critique peers. Students are often unaware how much their peers value meaningful reviews. A carefully constructed heuristic can guide students to provide an in-depth peer review that is valued, considered, and incorporated into the writer's subsequent drafts. A heuristic that guides a student to consider the structure of the argument, identify the rhetorical triangle, find the warrant, and look for conditions of rebuttal will remind students of the major elements of the argumentative essay.

The asynchronous discussion forum features of Blackboard and other course-management programs provide the time and flexibility needed to analyze and write a detailed peer review. Individuals in writing/peer-review groups of four (who share ideas for the invention phase of the essay) partner up, exchanging reviews. All four members of the group are able to read the papers and reviews of the other members in the discussion forum. After the online peer-review session, writers have time to revise their drafts for the next in-class peer-review session.

The in-class session features an entirely new group of four so that the writer has access to a variety of reviews. In the class session, individuals read their essays aloud. The importance of oral reading of essays has been explained by James Moffett:

> It is essential that [the student] address someone besides the English teacher and get some kind of feedback other than red marks. As one solution, I suggest that [students] be accustomed to write to the class peers as being the nearest thing to a contemporary world at large. Compositions should be read in class, and out of class, reacted to and discussed. One must know the effects of ones' rhetoric on someone who does not give grades and does not stand as an authority figure [. . .]. The issue here is not only one of cognitive development but of psychological independence. (248)

Students should be informed of the purpose and benefits of the oral reading of papers, because some students may not be accustomed to "performing" or having a "live" audience and might find this a daunting experience. After the paper has been read, the other three members give a round-robin review with a simplified heuristic designed to ensure that all four members of the group receive a review. This simplified heuristic might simply ask for strengths and possible revisions and/or a consideration of rhetorical appeals (ethos, pathos, and logos).

The online and classroom sessions provide the writer with four different reviews. Being exposed to two different groups, a total of eight individuals, provides a variety of experience and a greater opportunity for interpersonal relationships to develop.

A Sequence of Activities

The following sequence provides an inclusive explanation of activities that may take three to four weeks to complete, although teachers may decide to use only those activities that will be most useful for their students' particular writing projects. Again, it is not necessary for students to engage in these activities in class, particularly if teachers have access to course-management systems such as Blackboard, which easily facilitate online discussions.

As noted earlier, the groups should consist of at least three students so that each writer hears multiple perspectives from peers. Usually, the groups should include no more than four students, though, so that each student enjoys adequate feedback and sessions can be completed in a reasonable period of time. Here, then, is a general overview of the sequence. It can be modified to fit the kinds of writing that students are doing.

Session 1: The goal of this session is for peers to help a writer choose a topic that is interesting to the writer and that the writer can manage. The writer brings to the session several topics that he or she is considering for the project. Peers pose the following kinds of questions to the writer: Why are you considering this topic? How much do you care about this topic? What do you already know about this topic?

Session 2: The goal of this session is to help the writer begin developing the topic that he or she has chosen. The writer brings to the session some elaborated responses to the questions posed during the first meeting. In this second session, peers pose the following kinds of questions to the writer: What do you already know about this topic? What else would you most like to know?

Session 3: The writer brings to class some invention work for the project. Peers then help the writer consider ways to do further invention work and/or research. Peers also help the writer consider possible genres for the project—if the teacher has not specified a particular genre.

Session 4: This session is necessary only if the writer is constructing an explicit argument. The writer brings to the session a list of appeals—ethos, logos, pathos—that support the assertions he or she is making. Peers then help the writer generate counterarguments that readers might raise.

Session 5: This session is necessary only if Session 4 occurs. The writer brings a list of responses to the counterarguments that peers helped generate in that session. With the help of peers, the writer then decides how to address each of the counterarguments—acknowledge, concede, and/or refute. Peers also help the writer prioritize the list of counterarguments because it may not be possible to address all of them.

Session 6: The writer brings a full draft of the project to the session. Using criteria designed by the teacher and/or the full class, peers apply those criteria to the full draft.

Session 7: This session is necessary only if the writing project includes sources. In the session, peers focus on such matters as how appropriately the writer has quoted and/or paraphrased sources, punctuated quotations, documented sources, and formatted citations. It may seem like overkill to spend a whole peer-review session on these matters, but they are ones that many students find challenging.

Session 8: The writers bring to class revised versions of the writing project. Members of the peer group do round-robin editing of one another's papers.

Session 9: The writer brings to class the fully polished writing project to submit to the teacher. Before collecting the projects from students, the teacher asks each student to write for ten or fifteen minutes to reflect on the process of composing the project. This reflection can become part of the portfolio that the student is constructing for the course.

Addressing the Issue of Time in Peer Reviews

Although teachers may design effective peer-review sessions and questions, some students may be challenged by reviewing two or three papers in-depth during the given class period, and it may not be feasible for the teacher to extend the peer-review sessions because it may take away from class instruction time. One solution to this problem might be giving students the option of choosing the questions to respond to by asking them to consider addressing the ones that they feel will be most helpful to their partners when they revise their drafts. Another solution might be to ask students to take their peers' drafts home, so they can take as much time as they like to think and make constructive comments on the drafts. Students may either write their responses throughout the paper, or they may use the "file exchange" feature in Blackboard or other similar program to exchange their papers online.

After exposing students to three ways of providing feedback for their peers' drafts (for example, discussion boards, chat, and face-to-face), the teacher might request students' feedback on the advantages and disadvantages of these three approaches. The teacher might also ask students which one they would prefer for the next peer-review sessions. Students have a sense of which way works most effectively for them.

Conclusion

Collectively, these peer-review strategies enhance learning as students move away from traditional, solitary modes of writing, where neither strengths are enhanced nor weaknesses are addressed, to a collaborative approach that engages several cognitive processes, such as pooling information, questioning, clarifying objectives, planning, editing, negotiating conflict, giving and receiving feedback, and reflecting. As the essence of group work assumes active collaboration, students develop other important skills not required of them in a traditional lecture-style class, such as the careful listening necessary to provide critical feedback to their peers.

Although it does take time to prepare students to work together constructively and to implement the peer-review sessions, in the long run students will spend more time on task, will have fewer questions about the details of the final writing assignment, will feel more committed to their work, and will diversify their skills to meet the needs of the group. Overall, instructor time is spent more efficiently guiding peer groups to develop productive writing strategies at the outset, rather than correcting problems in the final assessment.

Work Cited

Moffett, James. "I, You, and It." *College Composition and Communication* 16 (1965): 243–48.

III Ideas for Evaluating Students' Writing

13 How Sharing Evaluation in the Writing Class Can Lighten the Paper Load

Allison D. Smith
Middle Tennessee State University

My first encounter with the substantial paper load possible in the writing classroom came as a high school teacher. Although I attempted to create a system that allowed students to improve their writing and also allowed me to grade and return papers in a reasonable amount of time, it was not until I returned to graduate school and became a teaching assistant in a first-year composition course that I began to learn that it was my planning and grading system that was creating the distressing and overwhelming paper load that I carried around with me into my office, my classroom, my car, and my home. In the required composition pedagogy seminar that I took in my first semester, I encountered a central philosophy that has stayed with me through the twenty years I have taught since. In that seminar, required reading included Erika Lindemann's *A Rhetoric for Writing Teachers* and her advice on handling the paper load. In the most recent edition of this classic text, she sums up her paper management guidance with this admonition:

> Teachers unwilling to share the authority face at least two unpleasant consequences. They feel obligated to mark too many papers (or to assign too little writing), and worse, they prevent their students from learning what the standards for effective writing are. Sharing responsibility for the paper load not only keeps us sane; it's also good teaching. (251)

Constructing an evaluation system within which students share their writing and writing assignments with one another and with you in a variety of ways fulfills two objectives: students get the chance to improve their writing by writing more and teachers lessen the paper load on themselves. Many overwhelmed teachers believe that they have to read and grade all the writing their students generate and often undervalue the significance of ungraded or informally graded low-stakes writing assignments. Low-stakes or less formal writing assignments give significant benefits, such as allowing students to "involve themselves more in the ideas or subject matter of a course" and ensuring "that students have *already* done lots of writing before we have to grade a high-stakes piece—so that they are already warmed up and more fluent in their writing" (Elbow 353).

The ability to recognize different levels of formality in writing is a skill that teachers can introduce to students early on; helping students to understand various levels of formality in evaluation is also a practical introduction for the classroom and the world outside. Since students come into class with preconceived ideas about what constitutes evaluation, each teacher needs to take the time at the beginning of the semester to explain the different types of evaluation possible for writing assignments. Letting students share in the metalanguage of evaluation gives them a head start on thinking about how to present their writing to the teacher and others. From the beginning of each writing assignment, students should know what to expect from you or others in feedback and evaluation. For instance, if you tell students that you will not be correcting specific local (grammatical or mechanical) errors in formal papers but giving them a general comment instead when local errors overwhelm the paper, they will not expect their errors to be corrected for them, and those students who want assistance will seek further help. After any kind of evaluation, the main goal is to "return the responsibility of the writing to the writer" (Gottschalk and Hjortshoj 59); this occurs with both informal and formal evaluation, whether the response is from a peer or the teacher. In fact, constant formal evaluation of both low-stakes (informal) and high-stakes (formal) writing assignments can stifle student creativity and enthusiasm, negatively affecting the writing and the writing experiences of students.

For different types of writing assignments (see Table 13.2), you can choose to share evaluation responsibilities by using any one of the valuable exchanges listed in Table 13.1.

Evaluation does not consist only of grading, but also of assessing, supporting, contributing, sharing, reacting, and ranking. Using a variety of writing and writing-evaluation practices allows teachers and students more opportunities to share and evaluate writing than using grades alone. In addition, a variety of shorter writing exercises can help

Table 13.1. Informal and formal evaluation possibilities

Informal Evaluation Possibilities:

- Do not check or collect the writing; use discussion, group work, conferences, or other means to encourage students to participate in ungraded writing opportunities.
- Have students exchange writing in class or online without your checking or collecting it.
- Use a check system to give credit for the work without reading it.
- Use a check system to give credit for the work and have students exchange the writing in class or online.
- Use a check system to give credit for the work, read it briefly, and respond orally in class.
- Use a check system to give credit for the work, read it briefly, and give short written comments.
- Use a check system to give credit for the work; have students exchange the writing in class or online and respond to the writing with their comments.
- Use a check system to give credit for the work, read it, and give extensive comments.
- Use a check system to give credit for the work, read it, and create a general comment sheet detailing common patterns and problems.[1]

Formal Evaluation/Grading Possibilities:

- Use a grading (A–F) system[2] for each work, read it, and give extensive comments.
- Use a grading (A–F) system for each work, read it, and respond through student-teacher conferences.
- Use a grading (A–F) system for each work, read all student papers, and create a general comment sheet detailing common patterns and problems.
- Use a grading (A-F) system for each work, read all papers, create a general comment sheet detailing common patterns and problems, and add two to three goal-related comments to individual papers.
- Use a grading (A-F) system for each work, read all papers, create a general comment sheet detailing common patterns and problems, and give extensive comments on individual papers.
- Use a grading (A-F) system for a body of work presented by students in a portfolio one or two times per semester.

teachers act more spontaneously when an instructional moment comes out of the blue; students can write immediately on a topic, and writing can be returned to students quickly, providing more opportunities for sharing, responding, and revising. The underlying goal for all assigned writing is to help students improve their writing; if you think of evaluation as never being the last word, "but as a part of a broader dialogue that might include discussion during or after class, email exchanges, or conferences" that all work together to improve student writing, then all levels of evaluation—including the kinds that lighten your load—work toward the overall instructional goal (Gottschalk and Hjortshoj 59).

Table 13.2 lists some of the types of writing that teachers can assign, along with common instructional goals and evaluation suggestions (see explanation in Table 13.1) that can lighten the paper load.

A writing teacher's life is chaotic and challenging, especially with the amount of paperwork that comes in and goes out on a daily basis. The best way to handle the paper load is to create an overall system that is organized based on instructional goals and sound teaching principles. The main goal that underpins all the work we do in the writing classroom is to improve student writing; be sure that each and every informal and formal assignment you give keeps this instructional goal at its center. Stephen Wilhoit's advice to new teaching assistants applies to all of us, no matter how long we have been teaching: get organized, set priorities, set goals, use time wisely, and combine tasks (18–21). Never forgetting that the goal of evaluation is not evaluation itself but the improvement of student writing will help us remember to use a variety of writing assignments and evaluation systems. One of the main advantages of keeping this in mind is the easing of our paper load.

Table 13.2. Types of writing and suggested evaluation

Type of Writing	Possible Length	Instructional Goal(s)	Suggested Writing Exchanges for Evaluation
Freewriting	1 paragraph to 1 page	Finding, focusing, or developing topics.	Informal
E-mail, chat-room, or discussion-board responses	1 sentence to 1 page	Sharing and exchanging information on topics or writing processes. Recognizing the need for assistance and seeking it.	Informal
Journal writing	1 to 2 pages	Finding, focusing, developing, or organizing topics.Sharing information on topics or writing processes.	Informal
Plans or proposals	1 page	Sharing information on topics, organization, or writing processes.	Informal
Lecture summaries	1 page	Sharing level of comprehension of important concepts.	Informal
Lecture responses	1 to 2 pages	Sharing level of comprehension of important concepts. Presenting questions, uncertainties, doubts, or problems.	Informal
Reading summaries	1 page	Sharing level of comprehension of important concepts.	Informal
Reading responses	1 to 2 pages	Sharing level of comprehension of important concepts. Presenting questions, uncertainties, doubts, or problems.	Informal
Position papers[3]	1 to 3 pages	Taking a stand on a topic. Sharing level of comprehension of important concepts. Presenting questions, uncertainties, doubts, or questions. Documenting source material.	Informal or formal
Handouts	1 to 2 pages	Presenting focused information to audiences.	Informal or formal
Research exercises[4]	1 to 3 pages	Locating, summarizing, and documenting authoritative sources on a focused topic.	Informal or formal
Research proposals[5]	1 to 2 pages	Identifying research questions and strategies for researching the questions and answers.	Informal or formal

continued on next page

Table 13.2. continued

Type of Writing	Possible Length	Instructional Goal(s)	Suggested Writing Exchanges for Evaluation
Evaluation documents	1 page	Evaluating writing on the global level (content, organization, and word choice) for self or peers. Presenting revision advice to self or peers.	Informal
Writing process summaries	1 page	Identifying and describing the processes used in writing.	Informal
Cover letters for papers or portfolios	1 page	Identifying and describing the processes used in writing. Identifying and describing strengths and weaknesses in own writing.	Informal
Quiz or test essays	1 to 3 pages	Sharing knowledge of focused topic. Organizing information in a readable and effective way.	Formal
Formal essay or research essay drafts	1 to 15 pages	Sharing knowledge of focused topic. Recognizing the need for audience evaluation or assistance and seeking it.	Informal
Formal essay or research essay assignments	2 to 15 pages	Sharing knowledge of focused topic. Organizing information in a readable and effective way. Showing awareness of purpose and audience. Demonstrating effective revision and editing skills.	Formal

Notes

1. See Gottschalk 58–59 for more information on creating a detailed general comment sheet.

2. The grading (A to F) system can be scored with or without a rubric or through analytical, holistic, or primary trait evaluation.

3. Gottschalk and Hjortshoj 150.

4. Gottschalk and Hjortshoj 150.

5. Gottschalk and Hjortshoj 150.

Works Cited

Elbow, Peter. *Everyone Can Write: Essays Toward a Hopeful Theory of Writing and Teaching Writing*. New York: Oxford UP, 2000.

Gottschalk, Katherine, and Keith Hjortshoj. *The Elements of Teaching Writing: A Resource for Instructors in All Disciplines*. Boston: Bedford, 2004.

Lindemann, Erika. *A Rhetoric for Writing Teachers*. 4th ed. New York: Oxford UP, 2001.

Wilhoit, Stephen W. *The Allyn and Bacon Teaching Assistant's Handbook: A Guide for Graduate Instructors of Writing and Literature*. New York: Longman, 2003.

Recommended Additional Readings

Connors, Robert J., and Andrea A. Lunsford. "Teachers' Rhetorical Comments on Student Papers." *College Composition and Communication* 44 (May 1993): 200–24.

Elbow, Peter, and Pat Belanoff. *Sharing and Responding*. New York: McGraw, 1999.

Fulwiler, Toby, and Robert Jones. "Assigning and Evaluating Transactional Writing." *The Allyn and Bacon Sourcebook for College Writing Teachers*. Ed. James C. McDonald. Boston: Allyn, 1996. 372–88.

Walvoord, Barbara E. Fassler. "Principles of Effective Response." *Helping Students Write Well: A Guide for Teachers in All Disciplines*. New York: MLA, 1986. 141–61.

Wolcott, Willa, with Sue M. Legg. *An Overview of Writing Assessment: Theory, Research, and Practice*. Urbana, IL: NCTE, 1998.

14 Reasons for Writing/Reasons for Grading: Conceptual Approaches for Processing Student Papers

William Broz
University of Northern Iowa

A s a high school and college writing and literature teacher, I invite each of my students to write many, many pages of formal and informal writing. In my own teaching philosophy, I follow the rule that all assigned student writing will in some concrete way generate credit toward students' grades for the courses. In my one-semester eleventh-grade composition course, students wrote fourteen short drafted and polished essays. In my high school American literature semester, students wrote from one hundred to two hundred pages of reading-response journal entries as well as fifteen brief drafted literary essays. In my college first-year writing class, students write three extensive (fifteen- to twenty-five-page) reading-response journals about the book-length texts we read, twelve shorter informal writings to support class discussion, and three major (six- to ten-page) fully drafted papers. The students in my college introduction to literature class write from sixty to one hundred fifty pages of reading-response journal entries, twenty-five shorter informal writings to support class discussion, and six two-to four-page literary essays. I use no tests of any kind in these classes. These writings, and the interpretive and composing processes that go into them, are the representation of student learning. Secondarily, the evaluation of these writings produces student grades.

This has been, of course, a large paper load for me. In a typical semester in high school, I had two sections of composition (700 papers total) and two or three sections of American literature, each with twenty-five students. (That's fifteen weekly "reading-response journals" and fifteen weekly literary essays each from seventy-five students, or around 2,250 papers.) Therefore, in a high school semester I could have had 2,950 individual student papers pass through my hands. A college semester often calls for me to meet thirty-five students in one section of Introduction to Literature (1,120 papers), twenty-five students in first-year composition (500 papers), and twenty-five upper-division composition students in one section of Writing the Personal Essay (900 papers). Therefore, in a typical college semester I might have 2,520 papers to deal with. Keep in mind that these totals include many pieces of informal "writing to learn" such as reading-response journals and one-page "discussion items" prepared by students for use in classroom discussions. Still, I have a lot of student papers to deal with.

Yet I can say that in my thirty years of teaching English I have never felt overburdened with student papers—burdened, yes; overburdened, no. I believe this is because I have been able to sort out in my own mind the differing kinds of response and processing (evaluating) that are appropriate for "writing to learn" and "writing to learn how to write." More important, I understand how my relationship to student writers changes depending on whether I am inviting writing, supporting writing-in-progress, or evaluating writing for a grade. These concepts covering the purposes for student writing and my role in evaluating it have evolved into a system for *processing* papers that allows me to survive, even (in my own mind, at least) thrive, while my students write and write and write. I believe the metaphor of processing is a useful one when confronting the evaluation end of paper loads. The discussion below outlines the thinking behind my processing of papers and offers glimpses of my actual practice. But because each of our teaching contexts is dynamically different, I cannot recommend *exactly* how you should handle *your* paper load; I can only share the conceptual thinking and my rules of thumb that have combined to keep me from being overburdened by my paper load.

My first suggestion is global and requires thinking before you invite students to write.

- Be clear on the purpose or purposes of the writing you assign and evaluate. Focus your response and evaluation primarily on the purpose of the writing.

In my English classes, grades 9 through 16, the writing that students do and that eventually finds its way into my "in" basket falls into two general classifications and one hybrid species. The first of these families is "writing to learn"; the second is "writing to learn how to write."

Writing to learn includes "reading-response journals" written while reading assigned texts, discussion items used by students to support small- and large-group class discussion, and single-draft writing exercises and exploratory writings assigned for the purpose of generating ideas for drafted works. These single-draft pieces of student writing make up the bulk of the student pieces I process.

Writing to learn how to write includes pieces taken through multiple drafts for which the student must generate a topic, develop that topic, and take the paper through at least two drafts (often several drafts), while revising and editing for clarity of meaning and conventionality of expression. These include all fully drafted pieces for composition classes.

Beyond these two kinds of writing, some English teachers also assign *writing for testing* in the form of timed or single-sitting essays, written primarily for the purpose of demonstrating knowledge of content, such as responses to essay-test questions.

Drafted, formal *essays about literature* form a special, hybrid classification for me. These papers embody some of the purposes of "writing to learn how to write" and some features of "writing for testing." As I will discuss in more depth below, my students usually take these papers through fewer drafts with less individual support from me, and I process them with less response and narrower and more mechanical evaluation procedures than I use with other "writing to learn how to write" papers.

Writing to Learn

The first reason for having these classifications clearly in mind is that most of the writing to learn travels from the "in" basket to the "out" basket with minimal or no response from me (beyond a brief review and the assignment of points or a grade). By minimal or no response in the evaluation process, I mean I put a grade or number of points on top of a reading-response journal without having made any other marks on the paper. And this minimal response in no way diminishes the importance or value of these writings for student learning. In my literature classes typically 30 to 40 percent of the credit for the course comes from these informal writings, which can account for 70 percent of the actual pages turned in. Yet all I ever do to evaluate these artifacts of student thinking and learning is to scan the pages while counting them and to affix a grade or number of points based on the general quality of the thinking they represent and the amount of writing the students do. For the reading-response journals I set a minimum page length which will assure a grade of C+, and I rank the As and Bs according to the number of pages, based on how the journals with more than the minimum number of pages bunch themselves up in each class set. In actual operation,

I sit at a large library table, flip through the pages of each journal, scanning while counting, and place the journals in piles in front of me according to the number of pages. Then I assign the most points to the journals in the stack with the highest number of pages and the next most points to the stack with the next highest number of pages. I can deal with a stack of 25 fifteen-page response journals from my college literature class in less than a half hour. It is my understanding of the purpose of "writing to learn" and my role as sponsor and valuer of such writing that makes this kind of cursory paper processing perfectly legitimate, even appropriate.

In my invitation to write reading-response journals, I tell students that the primary purposes of writing the journal are to facilitate engaged reading and to capture a record of their thinking while they are reading. This record will be the source for small-group discussion items and eventually paper topics for formal writing. Theoretically, I believe capturing response to reading as a resource for further thinking is the foundational operation of reader-response approaches to interpreting literature. Yes, there are a few things I need to do to ensure that writing these journals is a valuable experience for the students—offer occasional, in-class, directed journal-writing prompts designed to broaden student response strategies, make sure they are not simply summarizing the text (retelling the story), and check while scanning the finished journals to make sure that the kind of comments, questions, reactions, speculations, etc., that they put in their journals are, well, the kind of engaged thinking that is likely to lead to interesting understandings and interpretations and good literary essays. My evaluation of the general quality of the thinking is a simple up or down vote—"good enough" or "not good enough," the latter requiring the docking of a few points and a note about how to raise the journal entries to the "good enough" level. But my main function is to sponsor this kind of thinking on paper, to show the student how to use this thinking to develop more focused and mature interpretive opinions, and to give credit for this artifact of student thinking and learning.

Based on my invitation and the stated purposes for this "writing to learn," it is not appropriate or legitimate for me to note or evaluate any issues of correctness in the students' single-draft informal writing. Neither is it my place to evaluate any of the students' specific responses to the text. If I wanted to and had time, I could note a range of kinds of thinking represented in these informal writings, but that is more appropriately and easily done when reviewing the ideas students have culled from these journals for use in class discussion. It might be *nice* to respond to students' thinking in these journals, conduct a kind of informal chat or dialogue with each student, but that does not fit the purpose of the writing and would definitely be overburdening for me. Besides, I can and do use the journal content to coach selected students who are struggling to find paper topics. Conceptually, these journals represent *student* thinking so that *students* can use their own ideas to develop more mature interpretations. If I were to try to respond to these journals before students used them for discussion and paper topics, the time it would take me to handle the papers would interfere with the natural flow of the students' interpretive thinking. And besides, if I am going to go through their journals and respond to the entries that might be "good paper topics" (or to entries I think represent faulty readings), I might as well just lecture about the standard critical interpretations of the text and assign paper topics from the beginning. The students must learn how to use their own initial readings by having the chance to use them themselves. By assigning and giving credit for these journals, I am sponsoring students' interpretive processing. All I really need to do is to make sure they do it and give them credit for having done it. The feeling of obligation to respond to such journals in other ways (ways that are unnecessary) is, in my experience, the number-one reason offered by teachers for not sponsoring or not giving credit for this kind of writing. I handle writing exercises not taken beyond the first-draft stage and other writing to learn in composition classes in much the same manner—sponsor, acknowledge, give credit—but I don't muck around in it.

So my suggestions for responding to, and grading, informal "writing to learn" of the kind I have described above are:

- Value "writing to learn" by giving credit to students who have done it. If you do not value it, they won't, either.

- Review but do not comment on "writing to learn." These writings are artifacts of student learning which students will have already used to further their own thinking and learning by the time you process them.

- Evaluate "writing to learn" globally, based on the general quality of the thinking and the engagement in the task the writing represents. (Engagement in the task means the time and effort the writing represents—length and number of pages being the most overt indication of effort.)

- Totally ignore mechanical infelicities in "writing to learn." The students themselves are the only ones who have to really read these words and the only ones potentially inconvenienced by messiness or unconventionality.

A word about *writing for testing.* Because all of my classes are process-focused and process-based, and because my goal for students is that they gain greater facility with composing and interpreting processes, I have little occasion to ask students to write for testing purposes. But if I did, and if the testing situation called for students to write essay responses to test prompts in a single sitting in which time constraints and editing support would make it difficult or impossible for many students to display their knowledge of content *while also drafting and editing for correctness of surface features,* then I would process and grade those papers for content only.

Writing to Learn How to Write

My overriding strategy for managing response to and evaluation of drafted student writing in composition classes is to support student writing processes in ways that ensure the resultant papers are in the best shape possible before I respond to or evaluate them. That way the papers are much easier to respond to and evaluate, and the students have learned to function more independently while writing them.

Here are my suggestions for getting students to do most of the work in producing successful, drafted, polished papers in eleventh-grade composition, first-year composition, and personal-essay classes.

- Use class time for the periodic, peer sharing of drafts-in-progress.

Because drafting will lead to better papers, and because drafting is difficult and time-consuming, I always sponsor drafting by setting aside class time for the periodic, peer sharing of drafts-in-progress well before the final paper is due. I also "value" drafting by checking to make sure that students have drafts in class for peer sharing. Further, I make time for the peer sharing and celebrating of most finished pieces. Without any overt effort on my part, except planning and patience, this strategy allows the chance for self-expression and peer response to inspire students' own efforts toward better papers, papers that will be easier for me to process because they will contain fewer sites necessitating correction or suggestions for revision. At the same time, these strategies support collaboration among student writers, create an accessible and vital audience for students' writing, and foster community in my classroom.

- Value meaningful self-expression.

For students to fully engage in drafted, polished writing (thereby developing greater facility with all writing processes), the entire effort must have as its goal meaningful self-expression. If students are not trying to say something meaningful, then the writing, response, and grading are all a waste of time (see James Britton on "dummy runs"). This meaning making starts with the important writing processes of topic generation and topic development and results in making students responsible for all aspects of the writing process, including editing. Assignments in any genre, as long as the assignment and/or the conception of the genre are not too artificially or narrowly cast, can be vehicles for student meaning making and self-expression.

- Establish the classroom audience as the publication venue for (nearly) all finished pieces.

This is the simplest and most effective way to inspire competent self-editing and reduce surface errors, thereby reducing the amount of correction of such errors that teachers feel they have to do. Many students who do not mind looking dumb or sloppy in the teacher's eyes will do anything to avoid looking dumb or sloppy in the eyes of their peers, including proofreading and editing. Further, a vital and functioning audience of peer responders (not peer editors, checkers, or graders) will handle the lion's share of supportive response to content so I do not have to do it all myself.

These three suggestions can be summarized by recalling Mary Ellen Giacobbe's statement of three things that writers need: "time, ownership, and response"—rules of thumb brought to us by Nancie Atwell in *In the Middle*. Everything I can do to get the students to work as hard as possible on their papers *on their own* will make my job of processing easier.

This next, and very important, rule of thumb requires the philosophical stance laid out by Peter Elbow in "Embracing Contraries in the Teaching Process."

- Limit the amount of time you are in the evaluator role. Emphasize your coaching and collaboration role.

For me, there is a big difference in energy and attitude depending on whether I am supporting student progress toward a successful final draft or, in Elbow's terms, "gate-keeping," by trying to decide if a student writer should receive an A- or B+ for the quarter. Supportive coaching is invigorating and can be accomplished through marginal and summary responses to penultimate drafts or through writing conferences or miniconferences. Grading is draining and takes me to a lonely and institutional place that is not much like teaching.

- For papers that students take through a full drafting process, consider "due windows" rather than "due dates."

This can be important because in some schemes for classroom sharing, only so many final drafts can be shared each day, and those should be the ones that are truly ready. The others can have another day to grow and become more successful and more correct, and thereby easier to deal with. The teacher who can arrange "due windows" can deal with one-third of the class papers at a time over a three-day period instead of that foreboding, eight-hundred-pound gorilla, the *"class set."* More on grading below.

This is the most important rule:

- Never respond to the first drafts of pieces destined to be fully drafted, "writing to learn how to write" pieces. Except for consultations on topic development, respond only to the second-to-the-last drafts, the drafts in which, as Nancie Atwell says, the content is set and the students have revised and self-edited as best they can.

Unless you are sure that students have really done the best job they can on their own, do not hesitate to reject half-done drafts by saying, "This is not ready for me to read and respond to." If students have access to spell checkers and do not use them, do not accept their drafts. If you suspect that they have not seriously revised or self-edited, tell them they have not yet done their part.

But when you believe they have done the best they can on their own (and you have to be a believer to survive in this business), respond with written or spoken comments as the supportive coach, helping students toward the finish line. This is the time for teaching specific skills for which the draft provides evidence of deficiency. This is also the time for a bit of advice delivered in L. S. Vygotsky's "zone of proximal development," advice leading students to successful revisions and statements of meaning that their work-in-progress indicates they are moving toward, statements of meanings which they are "approximating" but have not reached on their own. This is also the time for gratuitous editing—helping writers approach, as much as possible, error-free writing. All of this is done in the name of collaboration and coaching—not in the name of evaluation and grading. In my composition classes, both in high school and in college, *every* formal, drafted paper gets a thorough response to the second-to-last draft, either in writing or in conference or both. Again, these efforts make evaluation and grading much easier, actually almost effortless, because after my response to the second-to-last draft, both I and the student will know what kind of "learning to write" the paper represents, and I will have nothing further to do in arriving at an evaluation mark than to put on my judging hat, read (or perhaps even just scan) the final draft one last time, and make a summary evaluation.

When you have in your hand a drafted student paper that is "finished," meaning that the student is not going to do any further drafting of the paper, follow this rule:

- Avoid extensive comments on final drafts made primarily to justify grading. A summary comment about the clarity and effectiveness of meaning will do.

If you must, go ahead and indulge yourself in marking a *few* truly egregious surface errors on final drafts (as well as checking "poor editing" on the evaluation instrument), but do not waste time and energy correcting errors or explaining corrections or explaining preferred revisions of content. Research clearly shows that these kinds of comments on students' final drafts are a waste of time because students do not have an immediate occasion to use or practice this instruction (Sommers). When you put this effort into the second-to-last draft, writers will use your advice and instruction, at least in the final draft. If they don't, you check the boxes—"inadequate revision" or "poor editing."

In fact, I advise teachers in classes focused on "writing to learn how to write" to follow the NCTE resolution of avoiding putting letter grades on individual pieces of student writing by grading on the basis of periodic portfolio or writing folder reviews. This is what I do in eleventh-grade composition and college writing classes. But this does not mean not evaluating pieces as you go through the semester. It just means not affixing a letter grade to individual final drafts. Feel free to evaluate using checklists, rubrics, six-, seven-, or eight-trait systems, or your own summary evaluation plan, any system which focuses primarily on meaning making and only secondarily on form and correctness. Students should be made aware of the evaluation system in advance. Just make sure your system is quick, easy, and holistic. Put the papers (as representative artifacts of learning to write) along with the summary evaluation in a folder for review at the marking periods. Leave letter grading until then.

Literary Essays in Literature Class

A review of the kinds and numbers of papers from my typical high school semester shows the importance of having an efficient and effective method for responding to and processing the essays students write in American literature class. Starting with a possible 2,950 papers for the semester, I know I am going to spend considerable time coaching and processing the 700 "writing to learn how to write" essays from two sections of eleventh-grade composition—in-depth written and oral responses to the second-to-last drafts of every paper. Of the 2,250 papers generated by three sections of American literature students, 1,125 of those will be the reading-response journals that meet with minimal or no response in the evaluation process. That leaves 1,125 literary essays (75 per week) of from one and a half to two and a half pages, for which the "final draft" is usually an edited second or third draft. For me, these papers are written for purposes that are part "writing to learn how to write *in this fairly narrow genre*," and part "writing for testing *the quality and development of students' abilities to interpret literature*." I hope lightning does not strike me, but I view the American literary canon as a kind of context for the student development of writing and interpretive abilities, and I view content knowledge of American authors and their works as a tertiary goal of minor importance.

Here is a brief review of my strategies for inviting, responding to, and evaluating literary essays in both high school and college. Most important, I view the writing of these essays as repeated chances to develop and demonstrate increasing facility for performing the same essential task—developing and expressing an interpretation of literature. In high school, students do this over and over again, fifteen times. They repeat the same processes six times in college literature class. For each performance, I support the interpretive process by requiring "writing to learn" as well as small- and large-group class discussion based on that "writing to learn." I support the composing process by sponsoring peer sharing of drafts-in-progress and peer response to, and celebration of, final drafts. With my overall daily, weekly, and semester paper load, I cannot respond to the drafts-in-progress of very many students' literary essays, only the drafts of students who are struggling and who seek extra help before and after school and during conference periods. (Some of these students send me drafts of their papers electronically for a quick response.) However, most students draft these papers with response from peers but not from me. Because most of the literary essays in my classes are written in response to common readings which follow a reading calendar, I do get class sets of these essays which I want to move into the "out" basket almost immediately ("in" on Friday, back "out" on Monday). So I read them, make a summary evaluation, writing only very brief comments on the papers, and assign letter grades, inviting any student who wants further consultation about the evaluation or grade to ask for a conference.

When I read the final drafts of literary essays to grade them, I am again at a large library table; I am again making piles of As, Bs, Cs. When I read and pile these papers, I am reading to determine three things that will be the basis of my evaluation (piling and grading) and response: (1) To what extent is this essay a well-expressed, well-developed interpretation of the literature? (2) Is this paper better than the one the student wrote last time, and to what degree does this essay represent growth and development of composing and/or interpretive processes? (3) Does the essay have major flaws in composing or interpretation that could be addressed in a brief coaching comment designed to move the student toward greater general success in the next essay? Such comments might include, "This thesis is too general. You need a more specific and focused thesis in your next essay." "You need more specific illustration of your point. Try using a quotation or referring to specific passages next time." These comments are more coaching for next time than specific justification for the grade on this essay. I do not take any time to correct surface errors, other than to say, "You are being docked one grade for weak editing" or to follow the rejecting rule for drafts that I suspect have not been edited and revised—"This essay is not ready for me to grade."

Some of the papers in the A pile would get no comment at all. Most of the students who wrote C or D essays get a brief, discreet, in-class or after-class verbal explanation of the coaching comments and a personal invitation to consult with me on the draft-in-progress for the upcoming essay. Because of the mix of "writing to learn" and "learning to write" papers, and because of the total number of papers in each of these literature sections, I do assign letter grades to every piece of student work and add things up at the marking periods in a pretty traditional way. (Portfolios at marking periods would contain too many sheets of paper to handle and I suspect that the bookkeeping for that many individual assignments would get out of hand if done only at marking periods.) However, because I see the "writing to learn" tasks as important primarily in service of the formal interpretive writing, the point value for the "writing to learn" diminishes over the course of the semester. Conversely, because I believe that I am promoting growth and development in both composing and interpreting, and that such growth will be developmental, incrementally over time, I begin the semester with lower point values for the essays and end the semester with significantly higher point values for the essays. Relative to each other, the grading value of the "writing to learn" is going down while the grading value of the essays is going up. I believe these evaluation strategies, along with the writers' repeated attempts to perform essentially the same task, support my students' growth and development of composing and interpretive processes in this narrow genre of the thesis/support literary essay while allowing me to survive this part of the paper load.

It may sound as if I am more of a writing teacher in dealing with my composition students than I am in dealing with my literature students. In composition class students are creating something out of nothing in a writing process that is more dynamic than the "school-writing" task in literature class. And again, teachers would not assign themselves fifty writing students and seventy-five literature students at one time. That situation represents an institutional constraint on our practices over which we have little control. Something has got to give, and in my classroom it is not going to be the occasions for students to read and write, nor will it be my sanity.

These suggestions remain at the level of principles of practice and general guidelines. They will require adaptation and development for implementation in specific classrooms, but that is the way with acquiring all good teaching practice.

Works Cited

Atwell, Nancie. *In the Middle: Writing, Reading, and Learning with Adolescents.* Portsmouth, NH: Boynton, 1987.

Britton, James N. *Language and Learning.* New York: Penguin, 1970.

Elbow, Peter. "Embracing Contraries in the Teaching Process." *College English* 45.4 (1983): 327–39.

Sommers, Nancy. "Responding to Student Writing." *College Composition and Communication* 33.2 (1982): 148–56.

Vygotsky, L. S. *Thought and Language.* Cambridge, MA: MIT P, 1986.

15 Evaluating the Writing of English Language Learners

Julie Ann Hagemann
DeVry University DuPage

Mainstream English language arts teachers often feel inadequately prepared to help the English language learners (ELLs) in their classes, especially when these students need a great deal of support in writing clear prose in English. On the one hand, they recognize that ELLs are like their native-speaking students (NSs), because first and foremost ELLs are writers who need the same kind of help *all* student writers need: thoughtful feedback on their ideas. On the other hand, ELLs are different in important ways. ELLs may not have the same cultural knowledge and language intuitions as NSs to guide their rhetorical and grammatical choices, so teachers need to develop special teaching strategies for them.

Having worked with ELLs for the past twenty years (both in traditional classrooms and in tutoring centers), I offer these suggestions to mainstream English language arts teachers who want to use sound strategies for evaluating the writing of their intermediate- and advanced-level ELLs. These strategies are based on the assumption that teachers will read and comment on several drafts of major writing assignments and that students will have the chance to revise their work before they hand it in for a grade. However, these recommendations might also help teachers weigh the impact of rhetorical shortcomings and grammatical errors on a student's grade—in those contexts where they can expect students to produce polished drafts of a writing assignment.

1. Match your expectations to the context of the assignment. Is the piece of writing a response to a major assignment, for which students have plenty of time to polish their drafts? Is it a response to an informal task, which students are expected to finish in a few minutes or by the end of the hour? Or is it, perhaps, a writing in response to a test question, which students are doing under time pressure? Obviously, the more time students have to work on a piece of writing, the clearer, more native-sounding it will be—and should be. Therefore, just as you'd do for your NS students, you should adjust your expectations of your ELLs to match the context in which they're writing.

In a testing situation, evaluate ELLs' answers by focusing mainly on global concerns, such as ideas, organization, and development. Do students seem to understand the concept addressed in the test question, even if they cannot express it very clearly? If so, consider giving them credit for their answers. If, however, the writing is so unclear you can't tell whether they understand the concept, consider calling them in for an oral exam. If they can express their ideas orally, then it's likely they know the concept. Like most students, ELLs generally feel more comfortable when they're talking about a topic than when they're writing about it.

2. Focus on the global before the local. Above all, ELLs are writers, and like NSs, they most need feedback on how effectively they're communicating their messages and meeting their readers' needs. So when you're reading the writing of ELLs, evaluate

- how clearly writers state their main ideas;
- how logically they organize their paragraphs;
- how sufficiently they develop and support their ideas; and
- how appropriately and accurately they cite their sources.

Focus your comments on one or two things the writer can do (in the next draft or in the next assignment) to present his or her ideas more successfully.

In my writing classes, all major assignments go through at least three drafts, and if possible, several conferences. This enables me to divide up my responses: I read the first draft for content and respond with questions that will help the writer generate content. Usually by the second draft, the content is fairly strong, so I can concentrate on local issues, such as grammar and sentence structure.

3. Develop a workable approach to helping ELL students reduce the number of errors in their writing. Once you've worked with ELLs to organize and develop their ideas, it's time to turn your—and their—attention to local errors. ELLs need to develop strategies for monitoring and correcting their own errors, with the long-term goal of improving the effectiveness of their writing. Like all writers, they want readers to focus on what they have to say, and one sure-fire way to do that is to reduce the number of distracting errors. Here's how I help ELLs deal with the errors in their writing.

Distinguish between errors that have an impact on meaning and those that are merely distracting. Some errors make the text difficult to read, while others are less noticeable. Errors that impede meaning are often errors in sentence structure, while errors that are merely distracting are often errors in word endings, especially when the rest of the sentence provides sufficient clues about what the writer meant. For example,

Errors That Impede Meaning	**Errors That Merely Annoy**
• The director uses lighting technique.	• The director uses many lighting technique.
Here the reader isn't sure of the meaning—does the writer mean one technique or many? Should the phrase read a lighting technique *or* lighting techniques?	*Here the missing* –s *on the word* technique *doesn't impede meaning because the reader knows from the context (from the word* many*) that the writer means more than one.*

I focus first on errors that impede meaning. As I'm reading a first draft, I put brackets around phrases or passages that I don't understand and indicate that in the margin. I ask "Did you mean . . .?" and try to restate what I think the writer meant in native-sounding prose. Then later, when I confer with the student, I start by asking about those marked passages. Ideally, we can together figure out how to express his or her ideas. I save distracting errors for another draft or another conference.

Distinguish between "treatable" and "nontreatable" errors. According to Dana Ferris, treatable errors are called such because it's fairly easy to articulate the grammar rules that apply in the particular context where the error appears. Moreover, these rules can be found easily in handbooks and grammar books and students can consult them if they're not sure of the rules. Nontreatable errors, on the other hand, are much more idiosyncratic; students have to use their intuitive knowledge of English to correct them. For example,

Treatable Errors	**Nontreatable Errors**
• My parent expect much of me.	• I enjoy to play tennis.
The missing –s *on* parent *is a treatable error because it's easy to*	*The incorrect verb phrase is a nontreatable error because it's not*

explain how to form plurals in English: in most cases, we add an –s or –es. Moreover, we know it should be parents, *because if it were singular, the writer would have written either* mother *or* father.

easy to explain why enjoy *takes a* verb + ing *structure rather than a* to + verb *structure.*

Note, however, that neither of these errors impedes meaning much. We know what the writer meant in each case.

My policy is to expect students, regardless of whether they're ELLs or NSs, to be responsible for identifying and correcting treatable errors, but I don't penalize them for nontreatable errors. Near the beginning of the term, when students are preparing to hand in the second draft of their first paper, I hand out a list of errors that I expect students to be responsible for. We review these errors in class, analyzing and correcting sample passages for practice. Then when I mark students' drafts, I merely underline treatable errors and focus my comments on nontreatable errors. As I do for errors that impede meaning, I write in a more native-sounding expression over a nontreatable error, and if possible try to explain my editing in the margins.

Here's the list of errors I expect my advanced ELLs to be responsible for; here too are the errors I directly correct for them:

Errors I Expect Students to Be Responsible For	Errors I Correct for Students
• verb tense and form • subject-verb agreement • plural and possessive noun endings • sentence fragments • run-ons and comma splices • some word-choice errors • punctuation, capitalization, spelling	• most word-choice errors • some pronoun and preposition usage • article usage • sentence structure

I've found that immigrant ELLs with many years of schooling in their home countries are more likely to have had formal grammar instruction, so they can often recite the treatable-error rules of formal English much more easily than can their NS counterparts or (immigrant) ELLs who grew up in the United States. On the other hand, these latter

ELLs and NSs are more likely to have intuitive knowledge of English, so they're better able to judge whether or not a passage "sounds right," and whether it needs to be edited for nontreatable errors.

Because nontreatable errors are idiosyncratic, some errors, such as a particular word choice, may come up only once or twice in the semester, so it's difficult to judge whether students have mastered that error. Other errors, however, such as preposition use, may come up several times. If this is the case, I encourage students to add this error to their personal proofreading log and to make it a goal to learn to see and correct it.

Help ELLs "see" their errors. Most people say they're much better at proofreading other people's writing than they are at proofreading their own. ELLs are no exception. Often, they can't see an error, but once you point it out, they'll know immediately how to correct it. I have a three-pronged approach for helping students notice their errors.

First, I help students develop their proofreading skills by explicitly talking about how to proofread. Most students don't realize they have to use a different strategy for proofreading from the one they use for understanding: namely, they have to slow down their reading enough to focus on each word (Madraso). When we read, we typically don't look at each word. Instead, we use our knowledge of the topic and of English grammar to predict what's likely to come. Then we glance at the text long enough to confirm it's what we predicted. When we proofread, on the other hand, we have to look at each word to judge whether it's a good word choice or a clearly expressed phrase, whether it's grammatical, and whether it's spelled and punctuated correctly. To better understand the difference between reading for understanding and reading for editing, I ask my students to read the following triangles:

It generally takes them two or three tries to notice that each triangle contains double articles. That's because at first they don't read each word. Rather they glance at the words long enough to recognize them as familiar stock phrases, so they assume they know what's written on the page. When students have to read them a second or third time, they tend to slow their reading down enough to really see what's there. We then talk about a number of ways students can use to slow down their reading.

Second, I've already mentioned how I discuss grammar and mechanics from the point of view of an editor, so students can develop their proofreading skills. Students learn the skills they practice, so when I hand out the error list near the beginning of the term, I present the errors in the form of proofreading lessons, adapting Neil Vail and Joseph Papenfuss's Daily Oral Language approach. After the initial lesson on proofreading, I often start class with a brief discussion of one or two passages of two to three sentences, each taken from students' papers or from the papers of former students. These passages focus on the treatable errors I want students to learn to see on their own.

Third, I minimally mark (Haswell) students' papers to help them see errors they may have missed on their own. When I'm reading second drafts of students' papers, I underline or circle words I want them to pay attention to. When I'm evaluating their writing electronically, I use the highlight function of my word-processing program to signal their errors. I don't explain what the errors are; I only give students clues about where to look. Students must figure out for themselves what the errors are and how to correct them. I find that minimal marking encourages students to take more responsibility for correcting their own errors.

Students have the opportunity to correct the errors before they turn in their final drafts. Most of the time, students see right away what revisions in grammar or punctuation they should make. For the other times, students can ask their peers or me for help.

Here's an example of how you can combine all three of these ideas into a policy for grading errors in ELL writing. It's based on a conference I had with an ELL named Danny, who had emigrated from Poland a few years earlier when he was a teenager and who had graduated from an American high school. He began an essay for his basic writing class with the following sentence:

Sands I was little boy, I alway dream to be good in karate.

I underlined *sands* and *alway* but did not comment on them. I thought Danny would figure out what conventions he had violated and make the corrections on his own. However, above the phrase *dream to be* I wrote in *have dreamed of being* because I knew that there were two nontreatable errors there that Danny probably couldn't correct on his own: (1) the idiom *dream of* and (2) the fact that *dream of* takes a *verb + ing* structure. Normally, I wouldn't correct verb tense—that's a treatable error—but I wrote in the correct tense because it was part of the idiom. Danny recognized the problem with *always* right away, but he had a question about *sands*. His way of pronouncing *since* made the *sands* spelling logical to him so he couldn't see it was wrong. I had to explicitly tell him how to spell *since*. Moreover, I explained (1) that English uses *of* with *dream* to talk about aspirations and (2) that *dream of* takes an *–ing* verb and not a *to + verb*. I told Danny I didn't know why—it just did! He'd just have to memorize how to use this verb and other phrasal verbs.

4. Ask students to keep a personal proofreading log. Different students—whether ELL or NS—have difficulty with different aspects of grammar, so I ask students to keep personal logs of grammar points that vex them. In their logs, I ask students to identify the problems, give examples of them and explain how to "see" them in their writing and correct them. I urge them to look at these logs when they're proofreading, so they look first for problems they're likely to have.

5. If your institution has a writing/tutoring center, encourage your students to get extra help with their writing. Tutors can spend additional, one-on-one conference time with both your ELLs and your NSs to help them develop their writing and proofreading skills in English. I find that students are more motivated to seek extra help when teachers offer them positive incentives, such as extra credit points.

Because ELLs share important similarities with NSs, English language arts teachers may already have more useful strategies to help ELLs improve their writing than they once thought. At the same time, ELLs are different from NSs in significant ways, and teachers have to develop new strategies to support these writers. Perhaps, however, the most important piece of advice in evaluating the writing of ELLs is this: Accentuate the positive and be tolerant of students' grammatical and sentence errors because with time many of those errors will disappear.

Works Cited

Ferris, Dana R. *Treatment of Error in Second Language Student Writing*. Ann Arbor: U of Michigan P, 2002.

Haswell, Richard H. "Minimal Marking." *College English* 45.6 (1983): 600–04.

Madraso, Jan. "Proofreading: The Skill We've Neglected to Teach." *English Journal* 82.2 (1993): 32–42.

Vail, Neil J., and Joseph F. Papenfuss. *Daily Oral Language*. Wilmington, MA: Great Source Education Group, 1989.

IV Ideas for Handling the Electronic Paper Load

16 Taming (Not Slaying) the Virtual Dragon: Handling the Electronic Paper Load

Lynne S. Viti
Wellesley College

Eighty percent of success is showing up.
                                        Woody Allen

Recently, I spent an hour and a half on the telephone with the customer service representative from my computer's manufacturer, troubleshooting a problem that I couldn't figure out, even with the skillful advice of our college's computer helpdesk staff. The pleasant, disembodied voice on the other end of the phone patiently led me through a complicated series of steps and helped me restore my computer to its functional state on the last day it had hummed along contentedly. From time to time, when one of the steps wouldn't work, the Voice would say, "Let me place you on hold, please, while I do some research on that." A few minutes later, he would return, prefacing his next round of instructions to me with, "I have done some research and have an answer for you." When the computer was fixed, I asked the Voice if I'd be able to replicate the many steps in this repair process should the problem occur again. He thought not, but encouraged me to call customer support again. I thanked him and hung up, knowing that in all likelihood, I would not be speaking again to him, but to another Voice.

This experience was eerily reminiscent of what passes for student-faculty interaction in the twenty-first century, especially now that many of us have successfully reduced the paper load by relying more and more on electronic communication to respond to student writing. With the rise of e-mail and the widespread popularity of software programs like First Class and Blackboard on college and university campuses, the convention of faculty office hours has noticeably declined (Wilson 10). Though we cannot lay all the blame at the feet of computers, it seems reasonable to conclude that e-mail and electronic bulletins have infiltrated our teaching and eclipsed old teaching practices now in danger of becoming extinct. At some institutions of higher learning, rhetoric or composition instructors required to observe office hours find themselves alone in front of their computers, responding to a barrage of student queries about required readings, paper assignments, and even fine points of grammar. Students who have grown up using Instant Messaging (IM) as a social tool since their middle school years bring their IM habit to college, and all too often enlist it for academic discourse without adequate guidance from faculty on when this is appropriate ("Letters").

This places the instructor in a difficult position, wanting to respond to students' electronically communicated requests for help with writing, but wary of increasing what can be called an electronic paper load and further diluting pedagogical energy. Faculty should stand firm against the onslaught of e-mail and document attachments, and revive the practice of sitting down at the table to talk with students about their writing. Over the past year, I have begun to use technology more judiciously. It does not mean I'm a Luddite if I refuse to read electronically transmitted drafts and return my comments to students by e-mail. It does not mean I am rejecting all academic uses of technology if I ask students to take advantage of my office hours, and to partake of the academic life through conversations about their writing.

The process that led me to this realization began in the mid-nineties, when I found myself spending more time in front of my computer than I had ever spent reading student papers or keeping busy office hours. I became quite familiar with my word processor's "track changes" editing function, oh-so-creatively color-coding my comments as I read and critiqued student drafts and returned these electronically. The more time I spent on the computer, both in my office, and at home— later and later into the night—the less time I spent at my office roundtable, working through writing issues with students. Real-time meetings with students—whether in my academic office, sitting down at the student union over coffee to discuss a piece of student writing, or responding to quick questions before or after class—had evaporated from my teaching life, replaced by e-communication. As well, my actual paper load appeared to decrease, but was supplanted by an even more daunting and ever-replicating e-load. After some soul-searching, I concluded that three essential stages of the writing process had been undermined by my embracing e-mail and electronic conferences in ways that were not pedagogically defensible. To combat and reverse this trend toward a kind of teaching that felt increasingly disembodied to me, I devised some modest solutions, perhaps more accurately characterized as *resolutions*.

Some Modest Resolutions

1. **Brainstorming and Finding a Topic:** Under the tyranny of the e-mail dragon, my students came less and less frequently to my office hours to brainstorm a paper. Instead, they would fire off e-mails suggesting the direction they planned to take in my assignment. Instead of asking students to hand in paper copies of thesis statements, or introductory paragraphs, as I had so often in the past, I had begun to let them drop their paragraphs into an electronic folder, and responded to these electronically as well. Dialogue between me and my students took place over e-mail, but the lack of synchronous discussion hampered us. And if we engaged in discussion by means of a computer chat function, I often found myself wishing I could shut down the computer and pick up the telephone, as the speed of IM and similar chat software makes it hard to reflect or pick up the nuances of a student's remark or question. Typical exchanges on Chat lasted a minute or two, no longer, leaving me more time to pore over e-drafts and get back to using those fancy color-coded edit functions in Word's tool menu. This made me wonder whether my students and I should not just admit to ourselves that we were fast becoming part of an online course.

Requiring three-minute conferences for brainstorming and paper planning addressed this problem, and cut down both on the paper load and the e-load. The venue for these varied—the classroom, before and after class, the hallway outside the classroom, the campus coffee bar, and my office.

2. **Feedback on First Drafts of Think-Pieces and Longer Essays:** By giving students extensive written comments on first drafts via e-mail or color-coded annotations in Word, but not seeing students in conference to talk about my appraisal of early versions of papers, I denied them the opportunity to solve writing and critical thinking issues present in their early drafts. I could no longer use the Socratic method to aid students in locating the solutions to writing questions. And I could certainly not read their spontaneous reactions, interpret their body language, or parse their questions as I was able to do in an office conference.

Consequently, I returned to the practice of first-draft office conferences, particularly for the first two essay assignments, limiting these meetings to fifteen minutes. If a paper had, in the words of my colleague

Winifred Wood, "misfired badly," I would ask the student how he or she might start over and usually would have her work one-on-one with one of our student tutors in the academic support center. I then would require a second revision conference a day or two later, and in that meeting, would focus on thesis, development of argument, use of evidence, and linking of evidence to claims the student was making in her essay.

3. Paper Post-Mortems: Even during those semesters when I used the computer most heavily to teach writing, I continued to rely on office hours almost exclusively to go over graded essays with students, both to explain my annotation system and to amplify my concluding comments.

Under my revised office-hour system, I ask students to bring—in addition to the graded paper—a list of questions about my comments. Additionally, a few days after I return each set of essays to students, I ask them to bring those graded papers with them to class. They then spend ten to fifteen minutes of class writing what I have them title "Feedback on Your Feedback." I ask them to address the following questions: Were all my comments clear? If not, which ones would you like me to clarify? What aspect of your writing would you most like to improve in your next paper? What part of this assignment gave you the most trouble? What, if anything, will you do differently when you approach the next essay assignment in this class? The feedback-on-feedback responses are one kind of "low-stakes" writing; they are ungraded, their sole purpose being to promote communication between me and the students. I read through these quickly and ask students to review them before writing their final feedback to me at the course's conclusion (Elbow 5).

Reviving students' participation in office hours is more than a practical way to reduce the e-load that we only pretended was reducing our paper load. It has the added benefit of teaching students how to engage in academic discourse. Particularly during their first and second years, students often avoid one-on-one discussion with professors, out of shyness or a belief that asking questions during faculty office hours shows weakness. The writing teacher promotes and models good academic citizenship by requiring students to show up and talk about their writing work.

The computer is a blessing in many ways—we no longer have to deal with erasable bond paper, correction fluid, or footnote anxiety. E-mail is a useful way to set up meetings, to answer small housekeeping questions, and to receive final papers from students. Virtual meetings are acceptable in the event of a snow emergency, or when a student has a family emergency and cannot fulfill all his or her academic obligations in person. Yet to use exclusively virtual communication is a poor substitute for the richness of the give-and-take we all value in our teaching work. In reducing the paper load, we must take great care not to replace it with an even more onerous virtual one, and to extinguish actual interaction with our students into the bargain.

Relying on Technology to Handle the Paper Load without Increasing the E-Load

In any course involving a considerable amount of student writing that an instructor is duty-bound to read and respond to in some fashion, computers and instructional technology can provide effective ways to reduce the paper load. Peer review of drafts and short writings sent by e-mail, closed discussion groups in the form of electronic bulletin boards or conferences, and asynchronous class discussions of readings and student writings—whether voluntary or required—can facilitate the creation of a learning community. All of these activities can take place outside formal class time, leaving precious class hours for lively workshopping of student writing and full-class discussion of assigned readings as well as student work. Asynchronous Q-and-A e-bulletin boards, such as "Ask the Professor" conferences, can be open only to students in a particular class. These provide a convenient place for questions ranging from the menial ("Do we have to include an audience description in Paper 2?") to the more complicated ("Does an article from the *New England Journal of Medicine* satisfy the assignment's requirement for a scholarly journal article in the field of bioethics?"). We can harness electronic media to expand each student's awareness of writing and required course readings, and to address legitimate, brief, and time-sensitive questions about the writing process. The instructor can set aside an e-mail hour every other day in which to read and respond quickly to short questions from students. Over time, this practice will provide a venue for recognizing student concerns and anxieties about writing assignments, yet subtly remind students that instructors are not on call twenty-four hours a day.

Revaluing the Role of Peer Tutors as a Counterbalance to Technology

Training our more experienced student writers to field questions, parse writing assignments, and vet paper drafts with novice writers is another time-tested way to manage the paper load. Giving these veteran student writers a title—student teaching assistants, writing tutors, or writing coaches—and a library corner in which to work, and paying them (even nominally), lends them authority. Students grappling with writing questions then perceive the tutors as legitimate, learned paraprofessionals in the writing community, and seek their help. In effect, incorporating student tutors into writing instruction provides yet another opportunity for personal communication, this time between tutor and student, about writing. Interposing a tutor between the student and the professor gives instructors more time to provide rich and meaningful written feedback on final drafts and portfolios, and to offer individualized attention and guidance to students during office hours.

Peter Elbow and others have described a range of activities for writing courses wherein students write to learn, but do not submit each assignment to the instructor for a detailed critique and evaluation. We can continue requiring these types of writing activities and harness technology to expedite the process by which students hand in such work, exchange it within editing groups, or post it on electronic class bulletin boards for the whole class to read and respond to—all of this without upping our paper or electronic load ("Letters").

By balancing the personal and the technological in our teaching, we can avoid paper fatigue as well as technological overload. By using technology selectively and taking care that it does not distance us from our students, we can nurture good writing practices and at the same time bring our students into fuller participation in the academic community.

Works Consulted

Connolly, Frank W. "My Students Don't Know What They're Missing." *Chronicle of Higher Education* 21 Dec. 2001: B5.

Elbow, Peter. "High Stakes and Low Stakes in Assigning and Responding to Writing." *Writing to Learn: Strategies for Assigning and Responding to Writing Across the Disciplines.* Ed. Mary Deane Sorcinelli and Peter Elbow. New Directions for Teaching and Learning 69. San Francisco: Jossey, 1997. 5–13.

Leibowitz, Wendy R. "Technology Transforms Writing and the Teaching of Writing." *Chronicle of Higher Education* 26 Nov. 1999: A67.

"Letters to the Editor: Answering All Your Students' E-Mail without Losing Your Mind." *Chronicle of Higher Education* 5 July 2002: 4.

Wilson, Robin. "A Kinder, Less Ambitious Professoriate." *Chronicle of Higher Education* 8 Nov. 2002: A10.

17 Saving Paper—and Grading—with Electronic Postings

Kimberlee Gillis-Bridges
University of Washington

As director of English Computer-Integrated Courses at my university, I incorporate technology into all my teaching, including literature, film, and cultural studies classes taught in lecture halls and writing courses held in computer labs. No matter the classroom environment, one technology remains constant: electronic postings.

I moved from paper journals to Web-based electronic postings in 1998. Prior to the shift, I had assigned journals that included responses to questions about course readings, expressive writing on issues related to upcoming essays, and quickwrites completed during class as catalysts for discussion. Although I collected journals only three or four times per term, offering even minimal responses constituted a significant workload. Moreover, my timing always seemed off. I found myself commenting on ideas that could have been fruitfully explored in discussions that had already taken place or essays that had already been submitted. I saw exchanges students didn't know they were having; in their journals, writers puzzled through similar issues or expressed opposite points of view, but solely to me rather than to one another. Since my own writing process depends upon continually engaging in dialogue with others, I wanted a way to bring students' hidden conversations into the open and to provide more opportunities for students to respond to one another as they explored ideas. Enter the electronic posting.

Students in my courses use a Web-based platform to make their postings. I employ a Web-based forum rather than an e-mail list because I want maximum flexibility in configuring my posting area. Typically, I shape posting boards around topics, with all posts related to a particular topic grouped together (see Figure 17.1). I also prefer Web-based programs because they give students a range of formatting options. Both Web Crossing, the program I used at the Claremont Colleges, and EPost, a tool developed by the Center for Teaching, Learning, and Technology

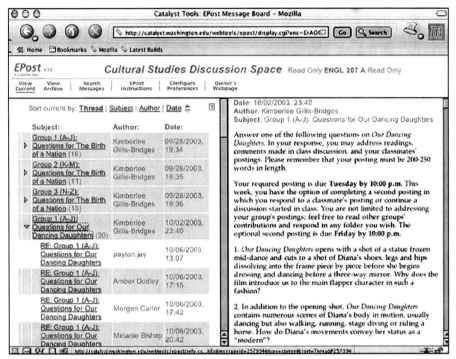

Figure 17.1. Screen shot of EPost posting board for English 207, Introduction to Cultural Studies

at the University of Washington, allow writers to italicize and underline text or to include hyperlinks to relevant resources in their postings. Web Crossing even lets authors upload an image, which appears beside their postings. Of course, Web Crossing and institutionally developed programs like EPost are not a teacher's only options. Many universities have adopted course management systems such as Blackboard and WebCT, both of which include Web-based discussion components.

Instead of having all students post into one topic area, I divide the class into groups of eight to twelve and ask each student to submit to his or her group's area a 200- to 250-word response to a question selected from a list I've posted. Questions require writers to do one of the tasks listed in Table 17.1.

I also give students the option to identify a key issue not addressed by my questions and to explain why the issue is important to the class's understanding of the text. Students may incorporate insights from lecture, class discussion, critical readings, or their peers' postings into their responses. I require students to post to the board once per week, with postings due the evening before class. While I do not assign a letter grade to the postings, students receive points for their work on a credit/no credit basis, with credit given to posts that meet the length requirement and demonstrate genuine engagement with the question. I have never had a student whose postings failed to meet the criteria for credit.

As I prepare my classes, I quickly read the postings to identify misunderstandings, areas of consensus and dissent, compelling arguments, or interpretations that raise insightful questions about the primary text or critical responses to that text. The postings provide a snapshot of students' current thinking, one I use to shape class activities. For example, I may begin class by calling on students who took different approaches to the same question and inviting them to summarize their postings. I then ask other class members which reading, if any, persuades them and why. If students tended to offer similar responses to a question, I describe the trends and have the class test their analysis by

Table 17.1

Task	Sample Questions
Analyze thematic or stylistic elements of a given novel or film.	Identify one key motif in *Dracula* and explain how it shapes the film's meanings.
Apply an argument made in lecture, a student presentation, or a critical text to a novel or film.	In class, we've discussed postmodernism as defined by Geyh, Leebron, and Levy and by McHale. Does "The Airborne Toxic Event" section of Don DeLillo's *White Noise* engage the ontological questions described by McHale? Does it exhibit the aspects of postmodernism defined by Geyh, Leebron, and Levy? In your answer, you may focus either on McHale or on Geyh, Leebron, and Levy.
Compare two or more course texts.	In our discussions of *The Birth of a Nation* and *Our Dancing Daughters*, we've analyzed the figures of the New Woman and the flapper. Does Saunders from *Mr. Smith Goes to Washington* represent a new female type, or do you see connections between her character and earlier "rebellious female" characters?
Examine a primary text through the lens of a question or issue explored over the term.	Is Shelley Jackson's *Patchwork Girl* a postmodern novel? Why or why not?

doing a close reading of a specific scene or passage. If students did not respond to particular questions, I focus class discussion on those questions, encouraging students to apply arguments made in their postings to unexplored territory.

My students and I also use the postings to work toward formal essays. I project excerpts from the class's postings and direct students to identify the claims writers have made and discuss how they might extend and support the arguments. Because the essays I assign often have a comparative focus, I ask students to analyze selected postings to determine whether the writer's interpretation of one text might apply to another. In a lecture hall, I make such inquiry a small-group project, giving each group a different posting to discuss and report on to the rest of the class. In a computer lab, I create new posting areas featuring excerpts from previous postings. Students then respond to three of the excerpts and attempt to extend the writer's arguments to another text. Toward the end of class, I give students time to print or save to disk postings they plan to reexamine as they develop their essays.

Electronic postings have reduced my grading time—I give points each week and ask students to respond to one another in class rather than writing brief comments on a weeks' worth of individual journal entries. However, the postings have also had other effects. Although I require students to post and read postings only within their groups, many students read other group's postings and include references to these postings in their own electronic responses or comment on them during class. Because all students must share their analyses via the posting space, they prove more willing to contribute to in-person discussions. The postings have thus allowed more voices to enter the class dialogue. Indeed, students have requested additional posting opportunities because of their desire to continue conversations with peers beyond class time. I now let students complete extra-credit postings in which they respond to their peers' ideas or expand upon discussions initiated in class. The postings have also had an impact on students' essays. As they post, students think in writing and produce texts that others can see, respond to, and incorporate into their own thinking and writing. Consequently, their paper drafts tend to have more clearly articulated ideas than those in the essays I received in courses that did not include the posting assignment. Moreover, students in my classes not only draw on their own postings in essays, but they also quote one another's postings. The act of engaging in frequent public writing has led my students to view their peers as authorities and audience. For this reason alone, I will continue to use electronic postings in my classes.

Works Cited

Geyh, Paula, Fred G. Leebron, and Andrew Levy. *Postmodern American Fiction: A Norton Anthology.* New York: Norton, 1997.

McHale, Brian. *Postmodernist Fiction.* London: Methuen, 1987.

18 Internet Grading: Following the Online (Paper) Trail

Helene Krauthamer
University of the District of Columbia

At the beginning of every semester teaching composition, I was one of those souls who enjoyed gathering my red pens, tan folders, and green grade book. I kept a folder for class handouts and another for student essays, which I carefully marked up with my red pens, recording all their grades in my grade book. Although I would encourage students to keep all the essays I returned to them, only a handful actually did or could find them when we held conferences. We would hold peer-review workshops by reading aloud essays to each other; we would hold grammar workshops by writing sentences on the board and then referring to grammar books and worksheets. When students submitted revisions, I had to cajole them to submit the originals as well, so I often had no idea whether or not they had paid any attention to my comments. At the end of each semester, I would print and photocopy a collection of the "best" student essays, which I would hurry to distribute to the students before the semester was over and the students scattered. Those, of course, were the old days, B.C. (before computers).

Now that computers have finally reached universities such as mine, where resources are tight, faculty are overworked, and students are stressed simply from daily life, we can all save a lot of ink, paper, and time, and perhaps do the job of teaching writing more effectively, with Internet grading. Internet grading can be defined as the use of the Internet to create and post assignments, submit and collect papers, grade and return papers, and keep records, all on the Internet. Those of us using course-delivery systems such as Blackboard find this to be a simple process, once the procedures are learned and practiced many times. The initial investment in learning this process is more than made up in the time saved while grading, and the convenience and learning outcomes are, as they say, priceless. When done well, this means no papers to collect, carry, copy, grade, or grieve over. For me, this means no more lost papers, no more wondering whether or not the comments written on earlier essays had any effect on later essays, no more guessing whether a student has progressed from Essay 1 to Essay 6. Internet grading can allow teachers to fully track student progress as well as the efficacy of their own instruction. Plus, it's fast, simple, and more efficient than traditional grading.

Background

Our university is fortunate to have a license to use Blackboard, Version 5.5, an online course-delivery portal, which provides the means to conduct virtually all class activities online. The classes I teach are mostly hybrid or Web-enhanced courses, meeting face to face for all class sessions but taking place in a computer lab at least once each week. The courses I teach are typically English Composition I or II, and the students are often first-generation college students attending this open-admissions, urban HBCU for the first time. Their ages and backgrounds may vary, but they are increasingly entering with more advanced technical skills, meaning that they are now more able to use word processing, e-mail, and attachment features than they were several years ago. I do not advertise my course in any particular way, and the classes typically have from twenty to thirty students each. Most students have access to computers, though these are often public computers in university labs or in their workplaces. Although some are scared at first, most are willing to learn, and at the beginning of each semester I hold a Blackboard orientation and provide them with a flyer containing detailed instructions on how to access Blackboard for course activities.

Methodology

First, I post the assignment in that area of Blackboard. It has been a very long time since I've made a trip to the copy center to duplicate worksheets for my students, and students never ask me any more what they are supposed to do. They know that everything is up on Blackboard. Using Blackboard, I have the option of posting all the assignments for the semester at once, or posting them as they are due. Typically, I post them as they are due so that students may focus on the newest task, often highlighting it in red, and then I leave everything up. I format the due date in bold, although I do allow late submissions. Clarifications or expansions of aspects of the assignment are easy to add when needed, and as the semester progresses students can easily see what the assignments have been and what needs to be done, since all are posted in one central area of the course. Having the assignment posted also allows me to copy and paste sections of the detailed instructions I provide directly into the student papers when I want to let students know they've omitted significant aspects. Also, I end each assignment with the grading rubric so that students will know specifically what they are to do. My rubrics for a course in English Composition I, for example, although they vary slightly for each assignment, generally consist of five parts, spelling out an easy acronym, TODUM: the existence and depth of the *thesis,* the appropriateness and coherence of the *organization,* the extent and relevance of the *development,* the accuracy of the *usage* (grammar), and the suitability of the *mechanics* (format), adding up to ten points (two for each category) for each essay. I can easily copy and paste the TODUM rubric from the assignment onto each essay that I grade.

I also add useful Web sites to each assignment, although I prefer to have students find Web sites for themselves. Web sites to help them with MLA style, for example, or those related to the theme of the assignment, or links to sites about writing are starting points and a useful list that I can often transfer to other courses or refer to myself. However, students can typically find even better Web resources when given the task, and I request that they post their findings in a discussion board area set up for the assignment.

Once students are working on their papers, I next set up the discussion board forum so that students can post their working drafts and get feedback from their peers, prior to actual submission. Students usually welcome the opportunity to read other papers and ask questions of one another. They can use the grading rubrics to provide one another with sample grades, and they can suggest useful Web sites to help one another do the assignments. Mostly, they can use the discussion board area to simply chat about the assignment and any problems they may have, allowing me insight into what may be causing them problems and giving me an opportunity to clarify murky points.

Using the Blackboard student drop box, students can quickly send me their assignments, when ready. If something is obviously wrong, such as a student's misunderstanding an assignment or omitting a significant portion, I can immediately e-mail him or her with more specific instructions. All the essays are stored in my drop box, where I can peruse them later to see whether students have made any progress over the semester. The essays are also stored in the students' drop boxes, creating quasi-portfolios for them. A submitted essay is never lost (although there has been no reduction in excuses for nonsubmission!), and it is particularly helpful to have essays this available when I hold conferences with students, which I do face to face, but in front of the computer.

Grading the essay becomes a simple matter of downloading the essay from my drop box in Blackboard onto my computer (left click, "save target as"), where I generally store it into the folder for the class under a file name consisting of the student's last name followed by the number of the assignment, e.g. smith1. However, if I am working on a public computer, I temporarily save the file onto the desktop and delete it when I leave. I generally never delete files from the Blackboard drop box, so there is no danger of losing the essays. Needless to add, I can access these papers wherever I go that has access to the Internet.

Using Microsoft Word, I then click on the "tools" option and select "track changes," then "highlight changes," and then check the box to track changes while editing. As I read the student's paper, I typically insert comments using brackets {} to set off my comments from the paper. Although the "track changes" feature also underlines the comments and places a vertical line in the margin to note the change, I use the brackets so that students cannot simply select "accept changes" for their revisions (one allowed for each essay) and will have to pay attention to the comments. Between the brackets, I identify the usage and mechanical errors I spot, not correcting them, just labeling them, e.g., {subject-verb error}. I can also easily copy and paste lengthy comments (e.g., "Please underline titles of books.") for each error as it occurs. I use the color highlight button to color sections of the text, the subject and the verb, for example, if I think the student may have problems identifying these, or a pronoun and its antecedent. It is possible to consistently color-code corrections—e.g., purple highlight for wordy sections, or green highlight for awkwardness—if this would be more eye-catching for the students. At the end of the paper, I insert the TODUM grading rubric with a summary of the reasons for the values and the grade. I then write detailed comments, sometimes copying and pasting problematic sections of the essay, and including hyperlinks for Web sites that would expand on my comments. A particularly useful tool is the Purdue Online Writing Lab (http://owl.english.purdue.edu) where there is a search box that allows the user to insert a topic (e.g., "commas") and find numerous links to pages of information and exercises on the topic.

After grading a set of essays, I create a list of the top ten errors the students have been making, with Web sites (often pages from the Purdue OWL) that could help them to improve. I post this list in a special "grammar workshop" discussion board area, inviting students to comment on whether or not these Web sites are helpful and to search for other useful sites. This is often an active computer workshop for students who enjoy surfing the Net, and they frequently find sites that I can use for other classes. Another computer activity is to ask students to post problematic sentences on the discussion board area and invite other students to revise them in a grammar-workshop approach. This allows students to see the many options they have when revising and to get feedback on their own suggestions.

A critical next step is to allow the students to revise their papers. The grade is then the average of the original submission and the revision, so that if a student earns a 7 on the original and then revises the paper so that it earns a 9 the grade would become an 8. Grading revisions is particularly easy, especially since it is no longer necessary to remind students to submit the original version along with the revised version, and comparing the two is an easy process by keeping both files open. When students have ignored comments made on the original, these may be copied and pasted, or highlighted, and brought again to their attention, saving me lots of time. I have often copied and pasted the entire rubric complete with my comments from the original to the revision, making only minor modifications where necessary. Generally, although the revised version may not be error-free, there are always fewer errors, and the subsequent new essays that the students write typically also show fewer errors.

I then conclude my comments section with my initials and the date. I rename and save the file adding "gr" to designate "graded" to the end, e.g., smith1gr. Next, I upload it into the drop box, send it to the student, and enter the grade in the grade book. If I want to see how the student has progressed from the previous assignments, I look in my drop box, or in my course folder, where all the papers, graded and un-graded, have been saved. Generally, the process goes quickly, averaging about twenty minutes per paper at the beginning of the semester and ten minutes by the end, which includes the return of the paper to the student. Traditional (paper) grading used to take me about thirty to forty-five minutes per paper at the beginning and twenty minutes by the end, not including the return of the paper, and then once I returned the papers to the students I had no records of my comments or their papers at all.

The final stage is to ask the authors of the "best" papers to post their essays in a special discussion board forum entitled "Best Essays" so that the other students in the class may read them and comment on them, thus giving more incentive for students to revise their papers and more models for them to follow. In the past, this form of "publication" took many days to prepare, and the students never had the opportunity to comment on one another's work as they do on the discussion board.

Discussion

The advantages of Internet grading are that I have continual access to all the student papers and if I have second thoughts about comments or grades I can make changes without messing them up. Knowing that I can revise my comments makes me more expressive, and I am actually less likely to provide the "cookie-cutter" comments that, I hate to admit, used to afflict me after lengthy hours of grading. Students, of course, appreciate the immediate feedback, and frequently the entire process of submission, feedback, revision, and resubmission takes place in a single afternoon. On a survey I e-mailed to them approximately two weeks after the conclusion of the class, the students reported being highly satisfied with this mode of grading, stating that they did check the Web sites, finding the Purdue OWL particularly helpful, when writing and revising their papers. They also appreciated the opportunity to revise their papers, and noted that they liked the speed with which their papers were graded.

Some of the drawbacks are that I never really know how many papers I have to grade until I go online and enter my drop box, and I must confess that I often go there dreading a big "stack" waiting for me to download. To overcome this, I try to grade papers at the same times each week, usually the night before class, and do a whole load at once, rather than peeking in every so often to see what I'll find. The process moves quickly *en masse*, and the comments I use for one paper are frequently applicable for others, although I try to resist the temptation to copy and paste comments from one paper to another. I do often, however, copy and paste useful Web sites, ultimately adding them to the list kept in the discussion board so that all may benefit. Sometimes the process of posting grades electronically is frustrating, particularly when the Internet connection is slow, and I think that it would be so much easier to simply write a grade in a paper grade book rather than to wait until the spreadsheet screen comes up. I also worry that the Internet connection may be unavailable just when I need it most, or that something may cause it to vanish altogether. As a form of insurance, however, I do print out the electronic grade book at significant points in the semester, notably the midterm and the final, and I keep student files on my hard drive, as well as in the drop box, although, really, the drop box may be safer. Perhaps the biggest disadvantage, if it is one, is that I find it harder to associate the paper with the person. Although the process of returning papers to students used to give me more opportunities to learn names, which are much harder for me to remember these days (would this be happening anyway?), this longer period of anonymity may perhaps keep my judgments about their writing more objective. The interpersonal connections are now created more through writing than through conversing, providing even more opportunities and incentive to write.

Conclusion

I can't imagine going back to paper, although I do keep a few red pens and folders handy, just in case. At the beginning of the semester there are still a few students who submit papers the traditional way, but they are the ones most eager to catch up with the others. I always schedule at least one class session per week in a computer lab to allow everyone, even those most intimidated by the computer, to learn the necessary skills: word processing, e-mail, and attachments. I give a computer-skills assessment survey at the beginning and end of each semester, and by the end there is always a big rise in self-rated skill level. The class retention level is also high.

Internet grading has become an essential part of teaching for me. Both the students and I have greater access to the assignments, their working drafts, resources to help them, their grades, and one another. Peer review has become far simpler than in the traditional classroom, as has access to supplemental instruction. Revision is easier than ever, and the students have more contact with me, as well as with their peers, than before. Publication is almost instantaneous, and students have student-generated models of good writing with feedback to refer to. Perhaps the biggest advantage for the writing class is that the writing opportunities are richer and more authentic.

My red pens, folders, and grade book are in great condition in their unused state, but I think my students are in even better shape with Internet grading!

19 Sharing the Fun—and the Paper Load: How E-Mail Can Help Middle Schoolers and Preservice Teachers Alike

Lauren G. McClanahan
Western Washington University

There are so many wonderful things about being an English/language arts teacher! First, there's the reading. As a middle school teacher, I loved guiding my eighth graders through the myriad worlds that were available to them through young adult fiction. Because I taught in a rural school district, the voyages we took vicariously through the characters in the books we read were often the only voyages my students were able to take, making them that much more valuable. And then there was the writing! How I loved to see my students' imaginations at work, starting with their own experiences and then gradually giving way to their fantasies and creativity. It was then, of course, that some logistical problems arose. Using a workshop approach helped, where my students learned to peer edit one another's work, but it wasn't until I began working with preservice teachers at the university level that I finally hit upon a way to lighten that paper load *and* use writing assessment as a teaching tool—all thanks to e-mail!

As a professor of secondary education, I am responsible for teaching several courses, my favorite of which is entitled Developmental Reading, Writing, and Learning in the Secondary School. In this course, it is my job to convince preservice teachers in *all* content areas that they, too, are teachers of reading and writing. This course does not focus on how to *teach* secondary students to read and write, but gives teachers strategies to use in their classrooms when they see students who are struggling to read and write at grade level. Sometimes this can be a hard sell, especially for my math and physical education students. Luckily, Washington state, and several other states throughout the Pacific Northwest, utilize a common language within which to talk about what constitutes "good" writing. Teachers in this region have narrowed what it takes to write an effective piece down to six traits: ideas, organization, voice, word choice, sentence fluency, and conventions. Recently, a seventh trait, presentation, has been added as an optional stylistic feature to be considered. Not all teachers use the same 6+1-Trait model of writing assessment—some use more traits, and some compress the list into four of five categories. However, most teachers involved with the creation of this assessment instrument agree that the above attributes are the foundation of what constitutes good writing, being careful to take grade level and the assigned task into consideration.

A Little Help from Our Friends

As much as I enjoyed teaching my preservice teachers about the language of the 6+1 Trait model of writing assessment, I felt that they needed more to make the ideas concrete, especially my students who were not going to be English teachers (my English teachers didn't need to be swayed!). This is where e-mail comes in. I decided to pair up with an eighth-grade teacher in Anchorage, Alaska, who was working on several writing projects with her students using the 6+1-Trait model. Deciding to have our classes work together was appealing in three ways. First, my students would get to work one-on-one with the eighth graders in Anchorage, helping them refine their writing according to the traits. Second, the eighth graders would be getting individual attention from someone other than their teacher, thus expanding their audience, and possibly their motivation to write well. Third, the teacher in Anchorage was now free from revising and editing over 150 papers a day, allowing her to act more as a mentor than an editor. The project promised to benefit everyone involved.

First, we had our students, both preservice teachers and eighth graders, write a brief letter of introduction to one another. My students began by telling their middle school partners a bit about themselves, their likes and dislikes, favorite authors, and a little about college life. I was thrilled to see how seriously my students took this introduction, and how nervous some of them were to make a good first impression! When my students were done composing their introductions (by a specific due date), they were to send them through their campus e-mail accounts to the main e-mail account of the eighth-grade teacher. Sending all of my student's responses through the teacher's account was a safety measure that we decided to take—a "filter" of sorts. When our eighth-grade partners received their messages, they, too, had a certain amount of time with which to respond. In this way, the project was kept on track, and no students on either side were disappointed by receiving late responses.

Once our eighth-grade partners received their introductory e-mails from my students, they had their chance to respond. The eighth graders introduced themselves, shared their likes and dislikes, and responded to what my college students had written. With this first response, the eighth-grade students also attached a piece of writing that they were currently working on. In the body of the e-mail, they told their university partner what specific traits to address in their editing. The eighth-grade teacher and I decided that rather than try to address each trait in each piece of writing, our focus would only be on two or three traits at a time, making the project a bit more manageable for each of us.

Once our eighth-grade partners sent us their pieces of writing, the fun began! Because they sent their writing to us as Microsoft Word attachments, we were able to utilize the "comment" feature under the "insert" toolbar at the top of our computer screens. This "comment" feature acts as a sticky note, allowing my students to highlight specific areas of their partner's texts. Once text is highlighted, the eighth-grade students need only pass their cursors over it and a comment from my students pops up. For example, one of my students might say to an eighth-grade partner, "I really like the way your voice comes through in this passage!" or, "I'm confused as to your word choice here—what alternatives could we come up with to make more of an impact?" Students on both sides of the project really enjoyed this feature, as it was easy to use and allowed them to make very specific comments. Another feature that my students appreciated throughout this project was the lack of paper involved—all work was done on the computer, thus literally reducing the paper load.

Everyone Benefits

Exchanges such as these went on throughout the quarter. In all, five exchanges were completed. When editing was complete on one piece of writing, another piece was introduced. Granted, this took some planning on the part of the eighth-grade teacher and me, but it was possible, and worked very well. Over the course of the ten weeks, friendships were forged, and some very helpful editing and revising had taken place. My students appreciated having "real" student texts to work with, and our eighth-grade partners appreciated having someone other than their teacher help to revise and edit their pieces. In fact, my students and I felt that because our partners had an "authentic" audience for whom to write, they took their writing more seriously. Their teacher agreed that her students wanted to put their best foot forward to impress their university partners.

After the project was over, and five complete exchanges had been evaluated, all of the students involved felt as if the dialogue had been positive. Not only did my preservice teachers appreciate working with authentic student texts, they also appreciated sharing their ideas and frustrations with other students in their content areas. One university student commented, "This project was much more helpful than just reading about the traits and then moving on. Now I feel as though I can actually apply them in my social studies classroom." Another student added, "This project was an eye-opener for me. I had no idea the range of skills that can be present in just one classroom. This is good for me to know before I have a classroom of my own."

The middle-school students also found value in the exchange. One eighth grader exclaimed, "This project was *awesome!* We got to help two people at once! Ourselves and our WWU partner. I think this project helped me understand the traits better because we were working one-on-one with another teacher." Helping the university students was a common theme in the eighth graders' responses. "I liked that we got a chance to escape from school to converse with a college student who is going to become a teacher." Another common theme was having someone other than their normal classroom teacher evaluating their writing. "I liked the extra input by people I don't know, because you are pretty sure that they're telling the truth." Another student said, "I liked this project, because someone else other than [my teacher] got to see my writing." Finally, one student summed up the project by saying, "The thing that I liked best about this project was that we could meet someone new, learn about their life at college, and actually e-mail. It wasn't just another writing assignment. We actually got to interact with someone, get their input on specific topics, and have fun with it, too!"

By far, the greatest complaint by all students was the lack of time. The middle school students especially wanted the exchanges to take place on a weekly basis, so that they could interact with their partners more often. The university students, too, wanted more time to practice honing their skills, and to just communicate with "real" students. My students and I agreed that the more experience they can get with actual students and actual student work, the more they will benefit in the future. Moreover, such projects are beneficial to practicing classroom teachers who struggle daily with the tremendous amount of paperwork they face. Working together on projects such as this, involving writing assignments in every content area, becomes fun for everyone involved! After all, why should English/language arts teachers have all the fun?

20 Share the Load, Share the Learning: Everyone Benefits from Online Response

Claire C. Lamonica
Illinois State University

Diane Walker
University High School, Normal, Illinois

Dear B—,
First let me say that your Halloween narrative brought back a lot of memories for me. As I was reading your piece I remembered having some of the same emotions as you did. I really liked how you kept describing all of the things that happened **before** *you could get to go trick or treating. This was a clever rhetorical device to use. By describing all of the events that led up to the actual trick-or-treating experience, [you made me feel] as if I too, was eagerly awaiting [. . .] the part where you guys got to go trick or treating. I felt your impatience and your excitement about Halloween. Some of the descriptions you provide here are nice—my favorites were your descriptions about the cool weather—the breeze, the day being "cloudy and cold." These add depth and color to your piece. Some suggestions for your next revision:*

- *Sometimes I felt as if you kind of got off track with the story—I was confused in some parts. In the beginning of your story you talk about wearing the "perfect" Halloween sweatshirt, but I didn't really understand what you meant by that until I read that paragraph a few times. I also didn't know why it was so important that your great-grandmother saw you at the Halloween parade.*
- *Dialogue is a great tool to use—many times it's better to include dialogue in a story rather than just tell your audience what happened. I felt the teacher's dialogue, though, was too long. You have her ramble a lot and I, as a reader, wasn't really that interested in what she was saying to the class.*

> • *I didn't know you were little when this happened until I had almost reached the bottom of page 1 of your narrative. I'm not sure how, exactly, you want to go about doing this, but maybe you won't throw your reader off so much if you clue us in—at the very beginning of the story—to your age when you had this Halloween adventure.*
> • *I love love love the fact that you put weather descriptions in this piece. But I want you to show me that it's cold rather than tell me. Don't tell me it's cold—I want you to show me that it's cold—were your fingers numb and tingly, was that breeze stinging your cheeks, were your toes feeling harder? You trick-or-treated in the snow—make us (your readers) cold with you!*
>
> *You've got a great start here, B—. Good luck with your revisions!*

The response above has much to recommend it. It is substantive. It is upbeat. It explains what the author of the original text has done well and how the reader responded to that, and it offers specific suggestions for revision as well as providing rationales for those suggestions. Most of all, though, it has this to recommend it: it *wasn't* written by B—'s English teacher. It was written, instead, by a student in a university methods class in the teaching of writing.

For three semesters now students in a Teaching of Writing course and those in a Sophomore Writing course at a local high school have been using an online discussion tool to communicate with each other on a regular basis. Generally, their interactions take a fairly standard form: the high school sophomores post drafts of their writing assignments to the discussion forum, and the university students respond to those drafts. Although not perfect, this opportunity for interaction has provided a number of benefits, not the least of which is providing the high school writing teacher with at least some help in "handling the paper load."

Why Online?

While technology does not actually make this project possible, it does make it more feasible. Since the high school where the Sophomore Writing class is taught is adjacent to the university, it would be possible for the two instructors to simply walk sets of papers back and forth across campus. To do so, however, would increase the turnaround time and diminish the effectiveness of the feedback. With technology, however, the fact that the two sets of students attend classes blocks apart is no longer an issue. In fact, the project would work just as well if the students were miles—or even states—apart.

In addition to minimizing geographical obstacles, having the students correspond electronically essentially removes time barriers, as well. The university students meet only three times each week, while the high school class meets every day. The university students meet in the morning; the high school students in the afternoon. None of this matters, though, in an electronic environment. The high school students can post their papers any time from any place they have Internet access. The college students can respond any time or from any place as well. The only restriction is that the university students are asked to respond within twenty-four hours of the high school students' postings.

Suggestions

Our collaboration on this project hasn't been without its difficulties, but over the course of the semesters we've worked together we've managed to address the most pressing of these, and we've discovered enough benefits to both the high school and the college students to convince us that we want to continue to work to improve the project. Based on our own experience with this project, we'd like to offer the following suggestions for designing an online partnership to help handle the paper load:

1. Identify a partner who shares your philosophy about the teaching of writing. The two of us who designed this project had worked together in a variety of settings long before we instituted the online partnership between our students. Those prior relationships had taught us a good deal about each other's strengths and quirks as professionals. Most important, however, we knew that we shared a philosophy that valued a process approach to writing, took into account the importance of multiple responses for every student engaged in that process, and encouraged responses that focused on different issues at different points in the process. This shared vision of writing instruction provided a strong foundation for our project.

2. Take time for technology. Any time a new technology is introduced into the classroom we need to take time to introduce it and allow students to adjust to using it. The technology for this project, while never really a stumbling block, was, from time to time, an irritant—primarily for the college students, as it turned out. (The sophomores, we observed, seemed much more adept at adapting to new technology and finding ways to circumvent it when problems proved temporarily insurmountable.) Still, anyone considering entering into an online response part-

nership should count on devoting a certain amount of class time to instruction and troubleshooting.

3. Set goals for the project. One of the first things we did after deciding to try this project was sit down and discuss what we hoped to gain from it. To be honest, helping the high school teacher handle the paper load was not our first priority. Instead, it was important to us that our respective sets of students gain valuable experience as writers and respondents. We wanted to make sure that both groups learned something about the value of peer response, that the university students learn how to provide helpful responses in their new role as emerging professionals, and that the high school sophomores discover the possibilities of substantive revision based on informed responses to their texts. Articulating a set of shared goals will help instructors design a project that is valuable for everyone involved.

4. Communicate about the writing assignments. At the start of the first year of the project, the methods students pointed out that it was difficult to comment on assignments for which another teacher had determined the parameters and evaluation criteria. While the classroom teacher knew how each unit was designed to function within the context of the course curriculum, the departmental scope and sequence, and the school culture, the online respondents were having to imagine or intuit this information. They knew that each task must focus on the development of certain skills and objectives, but it wasn't always clear what those were. This made it difficult to know what to look for or focus on when responding to their sophomores' drafts. The practice of having the classroom teacher provide a written explanation of the assignment, the goals of the unit, and the evaluation instrument or criteria before methods students responded to student drafts was quickly born of this difficulty and proved helpful in overcoming it.

5. Remember that it's a learning experience—for everyone! Even the most carefully crafted project will encounter difficulties and pose challenges for everyone concerned. Students, whether they are sixteen or twenty-two, are not always responsible for upholding their end of the bargain. Deadlines for writing assignments sometimes fall victim to the unexpected and have to be adjusted accordingly, throwing the calendars for both classes out of whack. Technology can run amok—networks go down, computers freeze up, disks get lost or damaged, word-processing programs prove incompatible.

Even when things appear to be going well on a logistical level, individual concerns can appear to threaten the success of the project.

Methods students making the transition from "peer respondent" in their own writing classes to "teaching candidate" in an online response project can suffer identity crises that make them feel insecure and threatened. Younger writers receiving responses from relative strangers can be frustrated or disheartened by the content (or lack thereof) and become unresponsive, failing to make substantive revisions even when the suggestions are sound. Even teachers can be thrown for a loop by occasional breakdowns in the process.

While such misadventures can prove frustrating for everyone involved, each provides its own opportunity for learning. It's important to remember this and keep the big picture in mind when relatively minor concerns threaten to become overwhelming.

6. Build in some bookkeeping time. While a project like this can, indeed, relieve the high school teacher of the need to respond to multiple drafts, tracking the posting of drafts, responses, and revisions was time-consuming for both instructors (although not as time-consuming as responding to twenty-five drafts!). Thus, the timely manner in which the students can receive their responses is, to some extent, offset by the time spent by the college and high school instructors ensuring that the process is moving along on schedule. Still, matters like determining whether the students had, in fact, posted their drafts and responses actually involve nothing more complicated than a little "bookkeeping," and the task of checking for postings could easily be carried out by a student or aide, leaving the instructors free to follow up with errant writers and respondents. Even in the worst-case scenario, although the instructors may not know until the completion of a given assignment that one or more students has failed to complete the task in a timely fashion, it's not the end of the world. Appropriate responses to such lapses can be determined and instituted, ranging from the natural consequences that arise when a writer fails to solicit and consider responses from other writers (that is, less effective texts) to more traditional consequences for incomplete work (point deductions, for example).

7. Show that you value the project. There's nothing more frustrating for a respondent than believing that the time he or she spent responding to a text was in vain, that the writer has not even considered making revisions based on the respondent's suggestions. Inexperienced writers, however, are often reluctant to revise their texts under any conditions and may well fail to do so unless they know that their teacher does, indeed, value not only the written product but also the writer's processes, including the revision process.

By the same token, methods students who see an online response project as "busy work" or an unwelcome addition to their hectic schedules may be reluctant to set aside time to provide substantive, helpful responses. Even more likely, under the pressure of time or uncertainty, they may resort to response practices that are less than effective. Thus they need to know that their instructor values both the response and the response process.

For these reasons, it is important for both instructors to demonstrate that they value this project and the experiences it offers their students. Such "valuing" may take the form of setting aside class time for the project, demonstrating that they are familiar with the work being accomplished through the project, demonstrating a willingness to help students shape their responses or revisions, discussing the progress of the project and demonstrating a willingness to adapt it to meet the needs of the students, and more.

8. Adapt, adapt, adapt. What we've described here is one possible iteration of an online response project that can be used to alleviate some of the paper load faced by writing teachers. While we've been generally satisfied with the results in our own classrooms, we have constantly reviewed and revised the project over the three semesters that we've been sharing it, and we will continue to adapt it based on our ongoing assessment of its effectiveness. Obviously, others should feel free—even compelled—to adapt the project to suit the needs of their own teaching situations. Identifying your own goals for a similar project may well help you determine the shape your particular approach needs to take.

9. Try it; you may like it! While we would be the first to admit that our online response project has not been without its challenges, we continue to believe that the benefits far outweigh the drawbacks. We encourage both high school and university instructors to seek out potential partners for similar projects. Whether those partners are across the street or across the country, implementing such collaborative projects can help you share, not only the load, but the learning.

21 "Dear Hamlet . . .": Student Letters the Teacher Never Answers

Todd Heyden
Pace University

As a college professor who has to publish as well as teach, I must allocate time for doing my own writing and for helping my first-year composition students do theirs. The discussion board (in, for example, Blackboard software) is a godsend because it allows me to efficiently monitor students' work at the same time that it permits them to learn to practice writing without me. I use the discussion board for informal writing that leads to formal essays. First, students write weekly letters to characters from assigned texts and post these on the discussion board. Then they send replies to peers' letters and receive answers regarding their own. Later, they use these letters and replies to generate essays whose ideas are richer as a result of students' having engaged in this ongoing "correspondence" with peers.

Pedagogically, the letters are highly effective informal writing tasks that build written fluency. My students lack the "muscles" that come with regular writing, and the letters provide much needed writing practice. This informal writing is also a crucial step in composing formal essays. For example, students write letters concerning *Hamlet* in order to prepare them to write an essay about the main character's inner conflict. The replies they receive to their letters broaden their perception of Hamlet's predicament and help them to go beyond simplistic judgments about his lack of resolve.

> Dear Hamlet,
> Lose the black clothes already, dude. That whole look does nothing for you. And stop moping around and acting weird. We all have to face the death of a parent. Why be such a momma's boy? Action is what is needed. Get on with it, or get thee to a therapist.
> Yours,
> Chen

> Dear Chen,
> You do not understand me at all. I am pretending to be crazy in order to find out the truth about my father's death. Therapy? When is the last time someone asked *you* to kill an uncle?
>
> I have thinking to do before I take action. Lastly, black is a very fashionable color, in case you didn't know.
> Later,
> Hamlet

The playfulness in the writing is indicative of the rapport that develops as students regularly correspond. When the author of the top letter composes his essay, his disapproval of Hamlet will be tempered by the knowledge that there are reasons for his apparent madness and indecisiveness. This will help him write a richer description of Hamlet's inner conflict. In another case, the letters can be a useful strategy for preparing students to write an argument essay. After reading *Harry Potter and the Sorcerer's Stone*, students must argue for or against the claim that the novel sends the wrong message to young women because it portrays Harry as an extraordinary, dynamic hero and Hermione as a mere clever helpmate. This prepares them to write an argument essay that contains a counterargument, something they otherwise find it difficult to create.

> Dear Harry Potter,
> People think you are such a hero, but they don't see how many times Hermione saves the day. Her skill at casting spells and her ability to think on her feet allow you to keep on looking like the hero, not to mention to keep on breathing. She deserves to be the star of the story more than you do.
> Best wishes,
> Ella

> Dear Ella,
> Clearly you have been reading too many books on feminist criticism or you would know that I am a very liberated boy. First of all, I *invite* Hermione to help investigate the sorcerer's stone. Secondly, anyone who reads the book can see we are equals. We treat each other with respect (based on your letter, this may be a new concept for you—ha!).
> Cheers,
> Harry Potter

When the author of the first letter writes her essay, she must include both her own opinion and a counterargument that acknowledges the point of view of her correspondent. This makes for a richer argument essay, one that looks at an issue from several perspectives and moves the student beyond reductive, either/or thinking.

I monitor the letters in two ways. The discussion board records the date and time each student posts, so I can easily ascertain if anyone has failed to do an assignment on time (late work receives no credit). Second, I randomly select student postings, photocopy these, and hand them out in class, such that students never know when their work is going to be featured. I do the same with responses to make certain that students are keeping up with their partners. I never respond in writing to their letters at any time during the semester. I especially like that the discussion board is an interactive medium because it promotes a sense of community among students in large classes. I create groups so that the same students write and respond to each other throughout the course. As the semester progresses, the discussion board becomes a "virtual student union" where they meet and learn online. In this way, I am not tied down to responding to all that students write, and they are not tied to me—they have writing partners with whom they can learn. In time, a student comes to see a peer, and not just the teacher, as a writing resource.

22 "Itching to Read It": The Online, Ungraded, Single-Paragraph Book Exchange

Judy Rowe Michaels
Princeton Day School, Princeton, New Jersey

When I get e-mail from my former students these days, most often they're writing me about "this really amazing book" they've just read. They think I should read it too. And then, if I'm lucky, three or four sentences appear on the screen telling me, quite specifically, why the book is so totally amazing.

Thirty years ago, as a beginning high school teacher with an M.A. in English and the New Criticism, I wanted all my students to fall in love with close reading of the chosen "texts" and then with writing the analytical essay. They suffered accordingly, and so did I. But over the years as I found myself reading—or skimming or browsing—new books and current magazines, rereading my old favorites, sporadically keeping a journal, and writing poems, memoir, and letters—some for publication—I realized that my priorities as a teacher had changed.

What I now care about most is helping students become lifelong and empathic readers. Carol Jago, in *Beyond Standards*, describes "compulsive readers" and "thoughtful readers." I want mine to be some kind of platonic cross between the two, but definitely open-minded and curious readers, who know what they like but are always willing to try something new. I want them able to reflect imaginatively on whatever they choose to read, and I want them eager to share their thoughts with somebody else.

I know that having my students write about what they read and about what their classmates are reading can help make all this happen. But I don't want to spend so much time with their writing that I have no time left for my own.

The arrival of computers in school and at home certainly offered new options for motivating and assessing student work. Recently I've found that the online classroom conference enables me to create a reading and writing community for each of my classes that takes relatively little time to maintain. The conference allows all of us, students and teacher, to exchange reading recommendations, to try to "sell" a book we love by offering specifics. In writing and reading single-paragraph recommendations, students begin to develop three skills they'll need for their longer, personal/analytical essays: forming a passionate, thoughtful opinion or thesis, choosing significant supporting details, and sustaining a clear focus.

Initially I set up the conference just to popularize—and enforce—our school's free-reading requirement (I know, "How can it be 'free' when we have to do it?") of one or more books per trimester and a minimum of four over the summer. But after a year's trial, I discovered what a good (and ungraded) writing exercise we had going. Brevity and a clearly defined purpose were two advantages, but authenticity of audience may have turned out to be the most important factor. An article in the "Circuits" section of the *New York Times* quotes ten-year-old Raya, a newly ardent writer: "I always wanted my work to be read by someone else [. . .] a regular person. With a teacher, it's their job. When someone else is reading it, they are doing it on their own free will" (Guernsey G1). Raya was posting her work and reading that of students around the country on a Scholastic.com site called Writing with Writers. But my high school writers appeared to find sufficient motivation in knowing that their own classmates would read their postings and might choose to write back. This is fortunate, because not only is my classroom not yet wired for Internet technology but also, as the *Times* notes, "online peer review [. . .] requires teachers to spend more time, not less, working with their students [. . .] they need to constantly monitor e-mail exchanges and online discussion spaces to ensure that students give good advice and are creating nurturing environments." For a variety of reasons, it's easier to do this monitoring when all the students involved in the exchange are one's own, and much easier when actual peer editing is not required.

I want my writers to experience first, right at the start of the year, the *desire* to respond to something a classmate has written. Choice is important here. It motivates them to read through various students' postings until they find a book that sounds good and an enthusiasm that's contagious. While they will, later in the year, actually edit one another's papers, at least for interest level, organization, and supporting evidence, their attention span and skills tend to be limited, particularly in editing analytical essays. Responding to the informal, one-paragraph recommendations out of personal interest, they soon realize that it was the recommender's choice of specific information, not just the book's subject, that drew them to write back.

And the respondee has a sense of accomplishment when her posting wins a new reader for "her" book. Asante wrote to Allissa, "Your first couple of sentences hooked me into wanting to read *The Color Purple*. You did a very good job of describing the book yet not giving it away. I might choose it as my next book." Mary Ellen also chose to write Allissa: "It seems like *The Color Purple* would be a book that makes you feel empowered, that you can do anything. It doesn't sound like a book that I would usually choose for myself, but now I want to find out how Celie overcomes all these hardships you mentioned." I think that for teenagers this kind of response matters more, at least initially, than any assessment I could offer. Allissa had entered our class with very little confidence in her writing, but these reactions to her first posting sparked an interest in developing as a writer. Gradually we discovered that her love of theater and experience as an actor enabled her to create effective monologues and dialogues. By the end of the year, she took the lead in both writing and staging her group's final exam performance.

These conference postings grow, in part, out of a classroom ambience that I try to create from the first week of school. Our English department has agreed that at least three class sessions per week, at every level, should start with five or ten minutes of free reading, for teacher as well as students, and we provide a yearly, annotated list of student and faculty recommendations. On my classroom shelves, I've gathered collections of poetry and short stories as well as literary magazines from various schools; these are available for in-class free reading when students forget to bring their current choice to class or decide they'd rather occupy these five-minute periods with shorter works. As people enter, they see me reading quietly, at my desk or in a corner on the floor; they generally settle in quickly. I can look unobtrusively around the circle to get a rough sense of who's reading what and how far along they've gotten. I ask them to keep their writer's notebook open in case they want to copy in a thought or phrase or word they've just run across. They notice that I'm doing this myself, and gradually develop the habit. Some days I make time for volunteers to share a passage or phrase they like.

By the end of the second week of school I assign the book postings:

> A. Next Monday, and then again at the end of each trimester (when we'll want ideas of what to read over vacations), please post *one*

fat paragraph, no more than half a page, describing and responding to a book you've read on your own during the summer (or the term). I'll do this also. If you want to address your paragraph to a certain kind of reader or to certain readers in our class, fine. The paragraph must describe, briefly, whichever aspects of the book—subject, characters, structure, language, point of view, ideas—strike you as important in conveying a sense of the book to the rest of us, but it must focus on those aspects that most affected you (perhaps negatively as well as positively). Think about this focus while you write your *thesis sentence(s). And when you finish writing your paragraph, reread to see whether you've maintained this focus.* You must include *two quotations* from the book to help give us a taste of the writing and to support your opinion. We're interested in *your own take* on the book, so don't rely on anyone else's; if you quote someone else's (including material from the jacket or foreword or the opinion of a friend), mention that person's name.

B. The day after we've posted recommendations, read at least *ten* of your classmates' entries. Then post a response to one person whose book interests you; write *three to five* sentences explaining *what interests you and why it does.* Notice some other classmates' responses: Any surprises?

Write informally, but proofread both your postings for clarity. I will not write corrections or suggestions; this is your final version. Reread the postings that seem strongest to you in order to figure out how you might make your next one even better. (Particularly notice how these writers are using quotations and incorporating them into their own sentences.)

When I go to the conference site, I enjoy learning about books that are new to me, seeing familiar ones through fresh eyes, and getting acquainted with my students' tastes. I enjoy seeing them take a genuine interest in what their classmates are reading. I enjoy not grading this writing. But as a writing teacher, I also appreciate how quickly I can spot which students know how to use specific details to support their impressions; which ones can shape a thesis sentence that will allow them to fit all their thoughts into one focused paragraph; and which ones know how to make smooth transitions between sentences. I can read these single paragraphs fast, perhaps record in my notebook a specific student's writing problem for future attention, and occasionally e-mail back a recommendation of my own—another book on a similar subject or by the same author. I don't have to print out, waste paper, lug home one more folder; I can deal with one class's postings in an hour after school and next day put in half an hour on their replies and an hour on another class's postings.

Scrolling through, I learn that ninth-grade Sarah, who's just finished T. H. White's *The Once and Future King*, has loved books about Arthur and Camelot ever since she was very young, and also that she likes learning new words. Perhaps I'll suggest that she try a book or two of Tennyson's "Idylls of the King." Sarah writes:

> When I picked up this book I thought it would be a hard one to understand and get through because the language just seemed too complicated. After reading the first pages, I began to pick up pieces of the story of Arthur and his knights that I had never heard before, that were exciting and new and funny. For example, I'd thought of Lancelot as always being handsome, but according to White, he was really "A rather sullen and unsatisfactory child, with an ugly face" (p. 320). As I progressed through the book, I began to like it more and more. Characters and feelings were explored and detailed to a point only equaled, in my opinion, in Marian Zimmer Bradley's *The Mists of Avalon*, also a book about the Arthur story except it only details the women's personalities. In reading White, I have developed a wanting to use big vocab words! There are some awesome descriptions that can sometimes only be well put with grand words: "The knights of the Round Table were sent out . . . and the choleric barons who lived by Fort Mayne took up their cudgels with the ferocity of despair" (p.355). Also "Often when the Queen was entertaining distinguished company under the flambeaux of the Great Hall, Lancelot had found Arthur sitting alone in a small room, knitting stockings." [. . .] Anyone who likes adventure, humor, and love combined with great words will really enjoy this book. Even if you think you won't enjoy it, give it a try. You might end up thinking it's the greatest thing since sliced bread, or maybe just the last good book that you read.

Later in the year, when we start writing poems, I discover that Sarah is one of the best poets in the class.

Zack, who recommended *The Mirror of Merlin*, wrote back to Sarah:

> *The Once and Future King* looks like something I would enjoy reading. From a young age, I have loved to read about the escapades of King Arthur, and I would love to continue reading about them. As well, it sounds like the great vocabulary would help me become a better reader and writer. Thanks for the good idea, Sarah!!

Ian responded to Zach's book on Merlin:

> I love science fiction and fantasy. Zachary's book interested me very much. I have read the first book of the Merlin series not knowing there were more. Zach's beautiful description compels

me to read the rest of the series. I hope I'll enjoy it as much as Zach has.

I remembered that Zach had chosen several quotations that created pictures of strange creatures on a magical island. Ian was responding to the book's style but as reflected in Zach's selection of favorite passages. Zach had written:

> Another thing that T. A. Barron does masterfully is create different cultures for every species he introduces, from the ballymag to the Scullyrumpus. Every species he creates has mannerisms, traditions, and a very detailed description of them. For example, the Scullyrumpus. "His small, furred head bobbed with laughter, causing his long ears to flap wide, revealing only three teeth, all of them green as his eyes." Although Barron does not go as far as fantasy mastermind J. R. R. Tolkien in creating entire languages, he does give each species certain slang or speech patterns that are uniquely theirs. "Haka-haka-tichhh. Poor lover manman! Lost his wittywits, he has. Now his balance, too!"

Ian was new to the school this year; Zach was a "lifer," here since kindergarten. I was glad they were getting acquainted this way—and, in fact, they soon became good friends.

Most of this first-year class in its first postings wrote four or five tiny paragraphs or three medium-sized ones. The idea that a single paragraph might go on for half a page and incorporate their reactions to plot, characters, and style was new to them. So, realizing that we'd have to spend some time on paragraph structure, I used a few of their postings, anonymously, as a classroom exercise: How could the writer create a thesis sentence capacious enough to allow her to include some detailed description of her book but narrow enough to focus us on her main reason for recommending it? This concept is a challenging one for ninth graders, especially when they're fresh from learning, in seventh or eighth grade, to write the *five*-paragraph essay—a structure that often requires little planning because the teacher has already done much of the work: "Find three pieces of evidence to prove that Tom Sawyer is . . . Offer three examples of how these two heroes are similar . . . Give three reasons why you think schools should not have dress codes . . . Write a brief introduction, a very short paragraph for each reason or example, then repeat what you're proving, and voila!" It's a useful format to master, but some students become so smitten with it that it's hard to lure them to more complex ways of thinking.

Actually, some of my first-year students' pieces were, potentially, a cohesive single paragraph; the writers just didn't realize this because they'd broken them up. Misha, posting on Jacqueline Woodson's biracial love story *If You Come Softly,* opened her six-paragraph piece with a thesis sentence that focused us right away on her main reason for recommending the book:

> Even though *If You Come Softly,* by Jacqueline Woodson, was written on a middle-school level, the message can be applied to any age: we shouldn't judge people simply based on the color of their skin.

This was her first paragraph. She then went on, in a new paragraph, to note how astonished she was by the fact that both the main characters were, like her, starting their first year at a private school—a point that just needed a little subordinating to her main idea about race to fit into a single-paragraph piece. Then she described, with two quotations, the two characters' situations and their story; next, the way Woodson creates suspense through structure and shifting points of view; and, finally, how the ending dramatizes that

> the world is not perfect. We cannot control the color of our skin or whom we fall in love with or when we die. The one perfect thing is the person that we finally, truly fall in love with; even if words and logic cannot be used to explain the reasoning behind our feelings.

Misha followed this with a concluding, one-sentence paragraph:

> Until racial and social equality are reached, Woodson's story can be used to show that something can come of two different people, and I would highly recommend it to anyone who is interested in this idea.

During class discussion, I suggested that the paragraph's line of thought needed a transition between love's illogicality and our present lack of racial and social equality. This idea led us away from our discussion of paragraph structure into one about biracial dating, a "digression" that ultimately helped Misha find a connection she could use to reach her concluding sentence.

More important, though, Misha had already heard online from Allissa and received her "grade":

> The book that caught my interest the most was *If You Come Softly.* I love how it's a mixture of romance, teenage life, and social and racial equality [. . .]. Misha does an excellent job describing in detail about the characters but leaves just enough out of the description to make me itch to read it. Thanks, Misha!

Works Cited

Guernsey, Lisa. "A Young Writers' Roundtable, via the Web." *New York Times* 14 Aug. 2003: G1.

Jago, Carol. *Beyond Standards: Excellence in the High School English Classroom.* Portsmouth, NH: Heinemann, 2001.

23 First There Is a Mountain: On Getting out of the Way of My Students' Learning

Richard Johnson
Kirkwood Community College

When I declared an English major in college, I had hoped my main job some day would be to read great works and talk about them. I wonder whether I would have chosen English had someone given me fair warning that I would instead spend most of my days reading not-so-great works and writing comments on them. In terms of sheer person-hours, marking student papers is typically the biggest part of an English teacher's job. And yet I don't remember ever taking a course in how to grade student papers. Was that part of our professional training? Was I just *gone* that day? I learned to do it, though, as perhaps we all did: nose to the grindstone, facing a fresh mountain of papers week after week. I tried to be Zen about it, which is always a sure sign that I'm having a lousy time. I kept up my own spirits with irony (another sure sign): as the piles of papers on my desk rose and fell and rose again I used to sing this old Donovan song from my youth, "First there is a mountain, then there is no mountain, then there is."

Before long, out of sheer necessity, I got pretty good at judging students' papers. I didn't think my students' papers were getting any better, but my *grading* of them was becoming exemplary—and why wouldn't it, since that's where most of my energies were going? As a consumer of my students' work, I was learning to internalize the standards of quality writing. I only wished the producers of that writing would do so as well. Since I only assigned as much as I could possibly grade, I became the bottleneck in my own classroom, the limiting factor in my students' education. I was, in a real sense, in the way of their learning.

And yet, truth to tell, these masochistic English teacher rituals had very little to do with how I myself actually learned to write.

The place I honestly learned to write—and learned to write honestly—was not in my high school English class but *after* school, among peers, working on the staff of the school newspaper. We weren't graded on the articles we wrote, and yet we wrote them with far more care than anything we ever handed in to a teacher. We wrote with a voluntary audience in mind (instead of a bleary-eyed English teacher compelled to suffer through every sentence, our audience was an entire school that might casually scan right past our precious words), and we wrote to satisfy the standards of our peers on the newspaper's editorial staff. They didn't grade our papers; they simply told us whether or not an article was ready for prime time. We learned to rewrite; we learned to cut. Deadlines were *deadlines*, not simply some English teacher's compulsive desire to receive a fresh mountain of papers all on the same day. We were writing for the school paper, but it somehow never seemed like we were writing *for school*.

I don't teach journalism. I teach ordinary first-year comp at a community college. But by rediscovering those long-ago lessons from my own high school newspaper days, I have transformed the environment in which my students learn how to write well—and I have changed forever my own ability to handle the paper load.

The key to the transformation was this: to get my students to stop thinking in terms of turning in their papers *to me*. Long ago, when I first began teaching, I tried publishing student work in our own little literary magazine. *Foxfire* it wasn't: copied, collated, folded, and staplebound. It was expensive and time-consuming, and too small to include a *range* of writing by each and every student. Publishing was just too much of a pain—until, that is, it became possible to publish online. Online publishing costs me nothing, but it allows me finally to teach writing the way I have always known I ought to teach it.

I announce to my first-year comp students on the very first day of the semester that we will be publishing an online magazine of their essays—personal narratives, profiles from the community, polemics on issues of concern to them. I will not be grading their papers, I tell them with suitable drama, and they stare at me, waiting for the other shoe to drop. The other shoe is this: they will have to write and revise their papers to suit the quality demands of their classmates. *Does that mean other students will be grading our papers?* No, not grading exactly, but other students *will* be telling you whether they believe your papers are *finished*—that is, ready for publication—or whether your papers still need some work. *But what if they just don't like my writing? Won't that hurt my grade?* Other students won't be deciding whether any paper *fails*; they will simply decide, as an editorial board, whether a draft needs further revision—and if they say it does, the writer can meet with me and re-write it as many times as it takes to satisfy its audience. That little matter of audience is key: students have been writing to please a teacher-audience since first grade, but I want my students to learn to write for a different audience: an audience of their peers, as represented by the class, and an audience of the world at large, as represented by the magazine's presence on the Internet. I want to wean them from writing for the teacher.

In practice, my classroom runs much like many other workshop-oriented composition courses, but with an added layer: after the small-group formative workshops that shepherd drafts through earlier revision, the whole-class editorial board serves as a kind of summative workshop of the final submission.

Deadlines are not deadlines *for me;* they are deadlines for their peers to consider their drafts and submissions. The formative workshops we do online through a class forum; students post a draft, and a small group of classmates respond with comments—praising some aspect of the draft, answering the writer's concerns about his or her own draft, and then asking her a few questions of their own. Later, after sufficient revisions, a paper is submitted to the whole class for approval to be published in the class magazine. If a paper is considered still in need of work, the process starts over—or ends right there if the writer chooses to abandon the draft.

If a paper *is* approved for publication, the writer submits it electronically—on a disk or as an e-mail attachment. I open the student's document, resave it as an html file, and link it to the online magazine. It's that simple. No copying, no collating, no folding, no stapling. Distributing the class magazine is as easy as posting it to the Web server.

My students have been writing *for teachers* as long as they've known how to write, and the only effect on an audience they have been hoping for all those years is to extract a decent grade from the teacher's carefully guarded hoard. But I come to work each day with the knowledge that I will be their *last* English teacher—even if they go on to become PhDs they won't have to take another comp class—and so I want to wean them from English teachers. I want them to internalize, for themselves, the standards of quality writing, as they learn to do by serving on the editorial board. I want to give them some initial experiences with the kind of writing that life after school will soon demand of them: writing to make themselves heard, writing to satisfy an audience of their peers, writing to elicit a response, writing to leave their mark on the world.

Editor

Jeffrey N. Golub, author, educator, and consultant, worked for thirteen years as associate professor of English education at the University of South Florida, preparing students who wished to teach English in the public schools. For twenty years previously, he had taught English, speech communication, and writing classes at both junior and senior high schools in Seattle, Washington. He has presented sessions and conducted workshops for teachers and school districts throughout the country on such topics as "Making Learning Happen," "Constructing an Interactive Classroom," "Infusing Technology into the Curriculum," "Developing Students' Speaking and Listening Skills," and "Responding to Poetry and Other Literature." Golub is the author of *Activities for an Interactive Classroom* and *Making Learning Happen,* two English methods texts; coeditor of *Reflective Activities: Helping Students Connect with Texts;* and the editor of *Activities to Promote Critical Thinking* and *Focus on Collaborative Learning.* In 1990, while teaching at Shorecrest High School in Seattle, he won the State Farm Insurance Company's "Good Neighbor" Award for innovative teaching, and in 1994 he was named one of the winners of USF's Teaching Excellence award. And he still loves chocolate.

Contributors

Rita Al-Abdullah has been a teaching associate at Arizona State University since 2004. She is working toward a PhD in rhetoric, composition, and linguistics. She was a participant in the first Athena Project to prepare teachers for the digital classroom at Arizona State University. Her research interests are Vygotsky, Bakhtin, and new media.

Allison Berg is associate professor of writing and American culture at James Madison College, Michigan State University. She is the author of *Mothering the Race: Women's Narratives of Reproduction, 1890–1930* and several articles on African American literature, popular culture, and pedagogy. Her current research focuses on literature of the civil rights movement.

Linda S. Bergmann, associate professor of English at Purdue University and director of the Purdue Writing Lab, has started Writing Across the Curriculum programs and writing centers at the University of Missouri–Rolla, the Illinois Institute of Technology, and Hiram College. Her teaching experience includes first-year composition; undergraduate courses in literature, pedagogy, and literacy; and graduate seminars in writing program administration. She has published articles in such journals as *Language and Learning Across the Disciplines, Feminist Teacher, A/B: Auto/Biography Studies*, and *American Studies*, and has written chapters on WAC and other aspects of teaching writing for various collections. She is currently coediting a collection of essays on the theoretical, curricular, and institutional relations between literature and composition, and completing a textbook on research writing.

William Broz is assistant professor of composition and English education in the Department of English Language and Literature at the University of Northern Iowa in Cedar Falls. His publications include *Teaching Writing Teachers of High School English and First-Year Composition* and articles on teaching English and writing in *Voices from the Middle*, the *Journal of Adolescent and Adult Literacy*, and *English Journal*, which in 2002 gave him the Edwin M. Hopkins Award for best article by a college professor over the previous two years. He is also a column editor for the *ALAN Review*. A lifelong Iowan, he taught high school English in eastern Iowa for twenty-five years, where both of his parents taught in one-room country schools for a time. He took his postsecondary education at the University of Iowa, an institution he regards as the cradle of writing pedagogy beginning with the publication of *Research in Written Composition* (Braddock, Lloyd-Jones, and Schoer) in 1963.

Karen Nilson D'Agostino teaches English at Brookdale Community College (New Jersey) and teacher preparation courses in the graduate school at Monmouth University. She completed her PhD at New York University and her MEd at Rutgers University, and her publications include articles and book chapters on teaching composition with technology and on computer classroom design. She served as a reviewer for the 2004 HP Technology for Teaching Higher Education Grant Initiative and serves on the editorial board for the *Journal of Research in Technology Education*. Her academic interests are teacher education, technology integration, and nature writing.

Ebru Erdem earned her master's degree in TESOL. She is currently pursuing her doctoral degree in rhetoric/composition and linguistics at Arizona State University, where she is also teaching composition and ESL in traditional and technology-enhanced classrooms. Her research interests are computers and composition and second language pedagogy.

Kimberlee Gillis-Bridges directs the English Computer-Integrated Courses program at the University of Washington, Seattle. Her teaching and research interests cover diverse areas of English studies—film, interdisciplinary writing, contemporary literature, and pedagogy. All her courses incorporate technology, with students using software and Web-based tools to develop their argumentative writing, textual analysis, critical thinking, and research skills. She has given multiple workshops and conference presentations on technology-based pedagogy. Her writing has appeared in the *Bedford Bibliography for Teachers of Basic Writing*.

Julie Ann Hagemann, a long-time teacher of writing to English language learners and basic writers, now directs the Academic Support Center at the DuPage campus of DeVry University in Addison, Illinois. She is the editor of *Teaching Grammar: A Reader and Workbook,* as well as several articles in *English Journal, English Education,* and elsewhere.

Todd Heyden is associate professor of English at Pace University in New York City, where he teaches composition and literature. He holds an MA in TESOL from the School for International Training and a PhD in English education from New York University. He has published articles on pedagogy in *English Journal, TESOL Journal, Teaching English in the Two-Year College, Academic Exchange Quarterly, The Journal of the Imagination in Language Learning,* and *ETC: A Journal of General Semantics.*

Ellen K. Johnson's teaching and research interests at Arizona State University revolve around the rhetoric of "things"—landscapes, fashion, decorative objects, jewelry, needlework, and numerous other belongings—as sources of insight about the meaning of Western literary texts. Her research in the field of rhetoric and composition focuses on the development and exploration of pedagogical practices appropriate for instructors transitioning from the face-to-face classroom to the computer-mediated, hybrid, and online classroom.

Richard Johnson studied English education at the University of Iowa. For many years he taught in both private and public high schools before accepting his current position at Kirkwood Community College in Iowa City, Iowa, where he teaches a full spectrum of writing courses, including developmental writing, English for nonnative speakers, first-year composition and rhetoric, a writing workshop in creative nonfiction, and a literature course on the essay. Professor Johnson supervises adjunct instructors and directs the campus's writing center. He also teaches a seminar in the University of Iowa's College of Education, and serves on the board of directors of Scattergood Friends School, a Quaker prep school. He recently published an article on Quaker pedagogy entitled "A Gathered Presence: Creating a Community of Conscience in the Composition Classroom," in *Minding the Light: Essays in Friendly Pedagogy*.

Helene Krauthamer is associate professor of English at the University of the District of Columbia in Washington, DC. She received an MA and a PhD in linguistics from the State University of New York at Buffalo and a BA in mathematics from New York University. She is the author of *Spoken Language Interference Patterns (SLIPs) in Written English*, published in 1999, and has published in *CEAMAGazine*, *Teaching English in the Two-Year College*, the *Journal of Teaching Writing*, *The Writing Lab Newsletter*, and *Linguistics*. Current research interests include assessment, electronic communication, and methods of teaching grammar.

Claire C. Lamonica is the associate director of writing programs at Illinois State University, where she teaches classes in writing and the teaching of writing. She also teaches summer school writing courses at University High School from time to time, and has nine years of experience teaching full-time at the high school level. She has a BS in English education from the University of Missouri at Columbia, an MA in English from Illinois State University, and a DA in English studies, also from Illinois State University.

Lauren G. McClanahan, a former middle school language arts teacher in rural North Carolina, instructs both undergraduate and graduate courses in incorporating literacy across the curriculum to preservice secondary education students in the Woodring College of Education at Western Washington University in Bellingham. She also serves as a supervisor for students completing their student-teaching internships at the middle and high school levels. Recently, her classes have partnered with middle school students in rural Alaska to discuss writing via e-mail. Lauren is also interested in how preservice teachers' dispositions can be analyzed through the use of writing as a reflective practice.

Barbara A. Mezeske is associate professor of English at Hope College in Holland, Michigan. She is coordinator of first-year composition and director of the Faculty Mentoring Program. In addition, she is a staff member of the college's teaching workshop for new faculty. Having spent seven years in the high school classroom before becoming a college professor, she has long been more interested in teaching and learning than in disciplinary specialization. She teaches expository writing, world literature surveys, the college's first-year seminar, and a course in paired novels. In 2000, she was a visiting scholar at Liverpool Hope University College in Liverpool, England, where she offered workshops on active learning, discussion, and writing strategies for the classroom.

Judy Rowe Michaels is artist-in-residence and coordinator of the Lively Arts program, K–12, at Princeton Day School, Princeton, New Jersey, where she also teaches high school English. She serves as a poet-in-the-schools for the Geraldine R. Dodge Foundation. She is the author of two books about teaching adolescents—*Risking Intensity: Reading and Writing Poetry with High School Students* and *Dancing With Words: Helping Students Love Language*—while her poems have appeared in many journals, among them *Poetry, Yankee, Poetry Northwest, The Women's Review of Books,* and *Calyx.* Her first collection of poems, *The Forest of Wild Hands,* was published in 2001. She has twice received poetry fellowships from the New Jersey State Council on the Arts.

Jennifer D. Morrison began writing at the age of eight when her grandmother gave her an old, clunky Royal typewriter. She became an English teacher after the princess-ballerina-astronaut concept failed to reach fruition. Somewhere within her thirteen years' teaching in public schools, the two passions merged, and she became a freelance writer for education. She is a National Board Certified Teacher (2000), has been published in *English Journal* and *Teachers' Digest,* and won the Paul and Kate Farmer Award for Writing Excellence in 2003. Currently, she serves as a Gifted Resource Teacher in Maryland.

Hillory Oakes is director of the Munn Writing Center at St. Lawrence University in Canton, New York. As a faculty member, she teaches courses in American literature, autobiography and memoir, advanced composition, composition and writing center theory, and English as a Second Language, as well as a tutoring practicum. She received a PhD in literary studies, with an emphasis in composition theory and rhetoric, from the University of Denver.

John A. Poole is currently assistant principal/language arts teacher at Hobbs Middle School in Shelley, Idaho. Previously, he taught English 9–12 at Hillcrest High School in Idaho Falls, Idaho. He is an adjunct faculty member at Brigham Young University–Idaho in both the teacher education and English departments. He has presented a multicultural program at the NCTE Annual Convention and is actively involved in multicultural issues.

Duane Roen is professor of English and head of Humanities, Arts, and English at Arizona State University East. In addition to six books, including *Strategies for Teaching First-Year Composition* (with Lauren Yena, Veronica Pantoja, Susan K. Miller, and Eric Waggoner), he has authored or coauthored more than 170 chapters, articles, and conference papers. He is currently working on *Writing for College, Writing for Life* with Greg Glau and Barry Maid.

Jennifer M. Santos is a graduate teaching associate at Arizona State University, where she has taught a variety of composition classes in online, hybrid, computer-mediated, and face-to-face settings. She is currently working on her PhD, specializing in nineteenth-century British literature. Her other interests include teaching with technology, rhetoric and composition, popular culture, twentieth-century British literature, postmodernism, and science fiction. She has presented papers in these areas at regional, national, and international conferences. Currently, she is coauthoring "Recomposing Religious Plotlines" with Keith D. Miller for *Negotiating Religious Faith in the Writing Classroom*.

Allison D. Smith received a BA in teaching language and composition, a secondary teaching credential, and an MA in applied linguistics from California State University, Long Beach, and a PhD in linguistics with an emphasis on writing and second language acquisition from the University of Illinois at Urbana-Champaign. She is currently associate professor of English and director of the writing program at Middle Tennessee State University, where she coordinates professional development courses for teaching assistants and oversees curricula for writing and writing pedagogy at all levels from first-year composition to doctoral studies in composition and language. Her recent articles have appeared in the *Journal of College Writing, English Leadership Quarterly,* and the *Encyclopedia of Linguistics.*

Lynne S. Viti, senior lecturer in the writing program at Wellesley College in Massachusetts, began her career as a high school English teacher. She later taught literature and writing at several colleges before embarking on a second profession as an attorney. She returned to academia on a part-time basis in 1987, teaching writing courses centered on legal studies, while working full-time as a trial attorney in Boston. Recently, she has directed her energies primarily toward teaching and writing. Her work in composition studies focuses on ways in which new technologies affect the teaching of writing, particularly with regard to plagiarism and students' legitimate uses of sources in their writing. Additionally, her fiction and poetry have appeared in several online publications.

Diane Walker has taught literature, writing, communications, and drama at University High School, Normal, Illinois, since 1986. She received a BS in theater education and an MS in communications from Illinois State

University. Areas of interest include teacher training, communication apprehension, reflective teaching and learning, alternative assessment, and technology and school development.

Ned B. Williams is originally from southern Idaho, but now, after twenty-five years, claims Laie, Hawaii, as his home. He graduated with degrees from the University of Idaho, Brigham Young University–Provo, and the University at Wisconsin–Milwaukee. He has been a faculty member at Brigham Young University–Hawaii since 1977, except for two years as a PhD student (Wisconsin), two years as an exchange professor (Provo), and two years on leave (Switzerland). Currently, he is serving as chair of the Department of English. Ned has published plays and several short stories as well as a number of critical articles. His latest publications include a series of articles regarding research in the pharmaceutical industry.

Patricia S. Williams received her undergraduate degree from Salve Regina University in Newport and a master's degree from Providence College and did additional postgraduate work at Catholic University in Washington, DC, the University of Rhode Island, and Tufts University in Boston. She has enjoyed an extremely satisfying and exciting teaching career for over thirty-five years, the last thirty years having been spent at St. Mary Academy–Bay View, where she has served as English department chair in addition to teaching duties. For ten years she coached a highly successful academic decathlon team and currently serves as advisor to the senior class.

Lauren Yena is a doctoral candidate in rhetoric and composition at Arizona State University, where she has served as assistant to the director of writing programs and co-director of an Athena Project Grant designed to facilitate teachers' transitions into computer-mediated writing classrooms. She has taught writing and literature in universities, community colleges, and high schools since 1994. Her current research interests include secondary and postsecondary writing pedagogy and assessment, university-based literacy outreach programs, and technology-mediated writing instruction. She is coeditor of *Strategies for Teaching First-Year Composition* (with Duane Roen, Veronica Pantoja, Susan K. Miller, and Eric Waggoner) and has contributed to *Computers and Composition Online* and the Stairwell, an online forum in the e-journal *Lore*.

This book was typeset in Palatino and Helvetica by Electronic Imaging.
Typefaces used on the cover were BankGothic, Frutiger, and Arquitectura.
The book was printed on 60-lb. Williamsburg Offset paper
by Versa Press, Inc.